# 22

## A Poetimagery Book

# Zuqy

## The Decennium Series

### Volume Two

Zmurbi Librumz

Zmurbi Librumz
2011

Front Cover Design: Octorafy
Interior Design: Octorafy
Photography: Zuqy

Poetry & Photography With Love From Illinois.

For Dad... Thank you for the music and art

For Mom... Thank you for the might and heart

For Bee... Thank you for the memories and laughter

For Jack... Thank you for the magic and adventures

But most of all...

Thank you for the love...

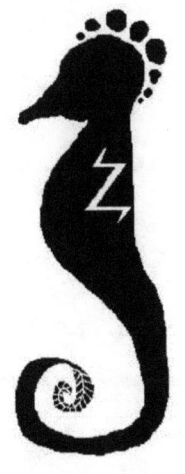

# Contents

Ruof

X Y To The Z

Portrait Pensive

X Y Equals Z

Intermissio

X Y & Z

These Twentyish Thoughts

Summer Starlight

The Octorafy Gallery
EST. 02022002
#ImageryGallery

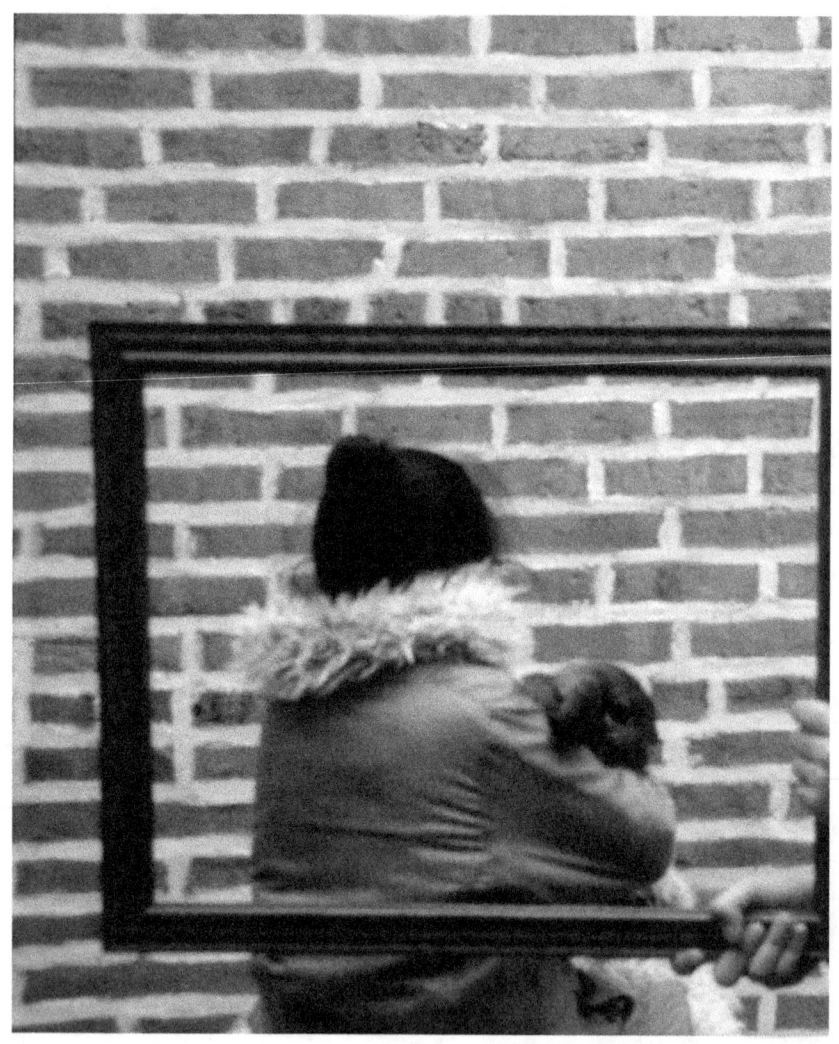

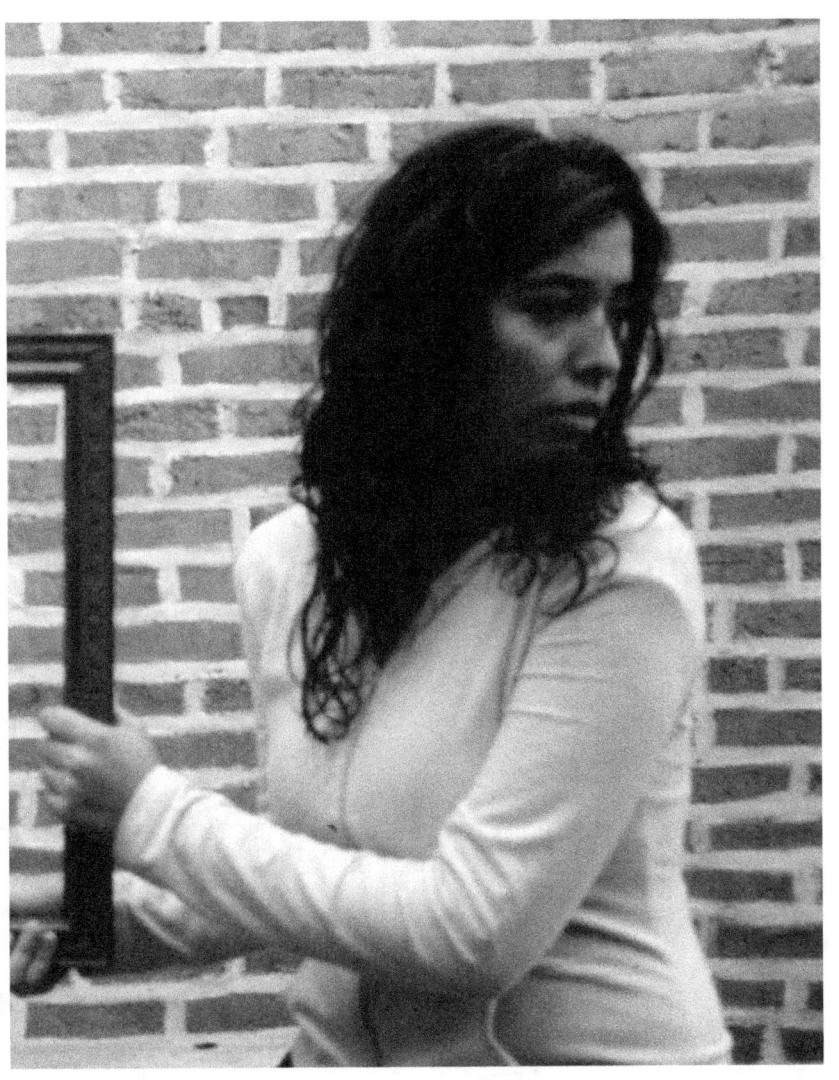

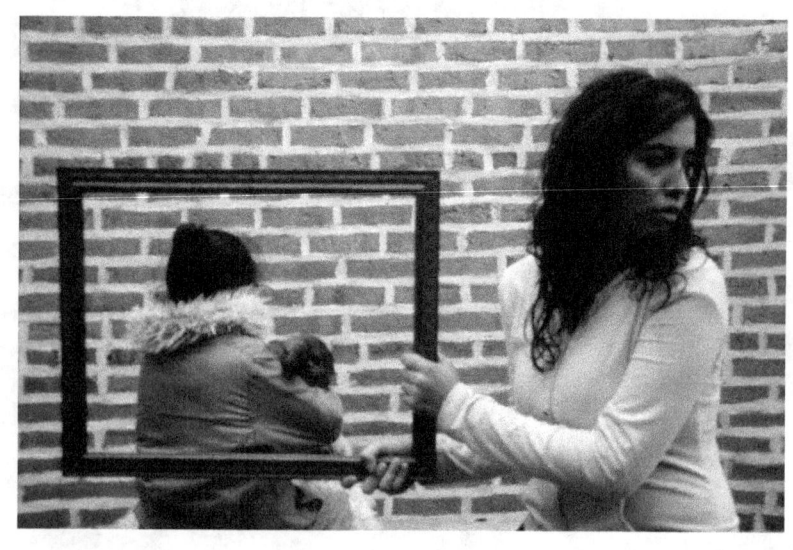

# "First Frame"

# Illinois

# Autumn

# 2005

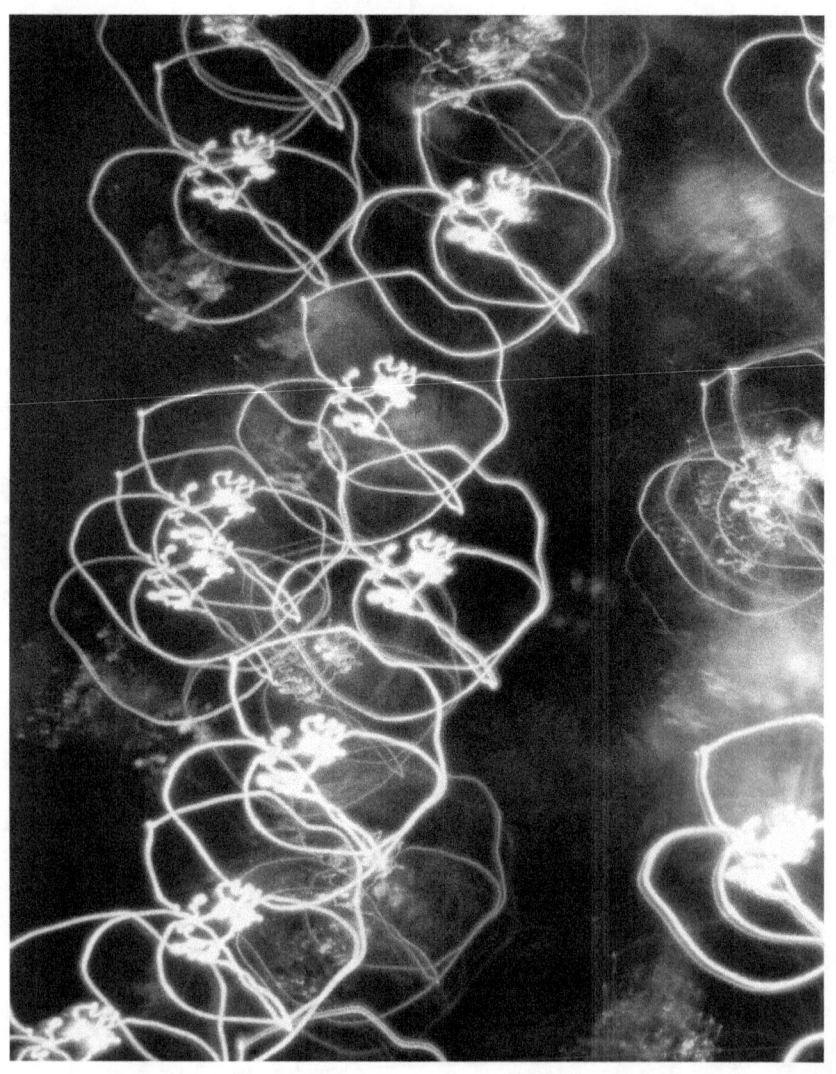

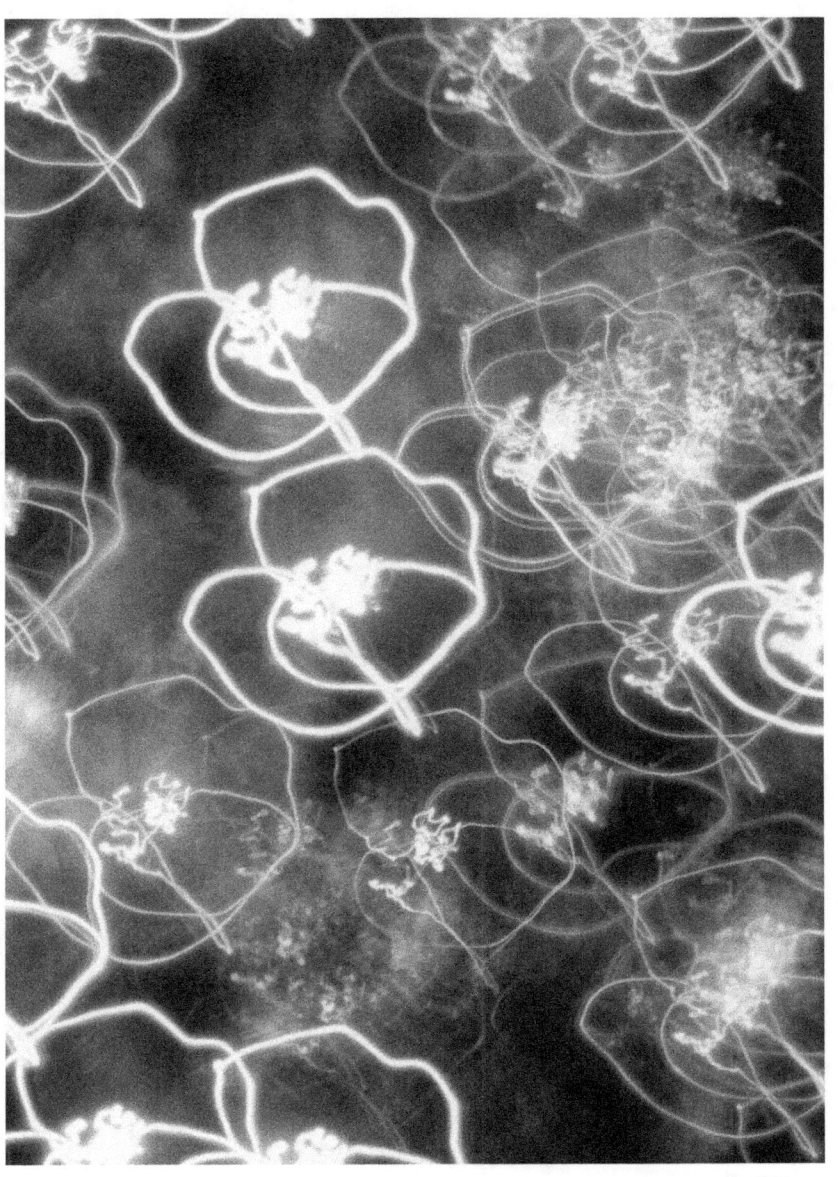

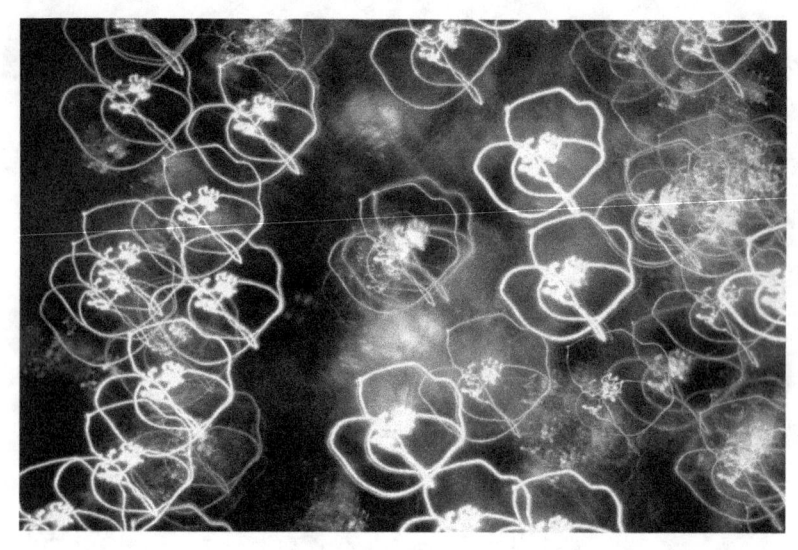

"Ocean Orchid"

# Illinois
# Autumn
# 2006

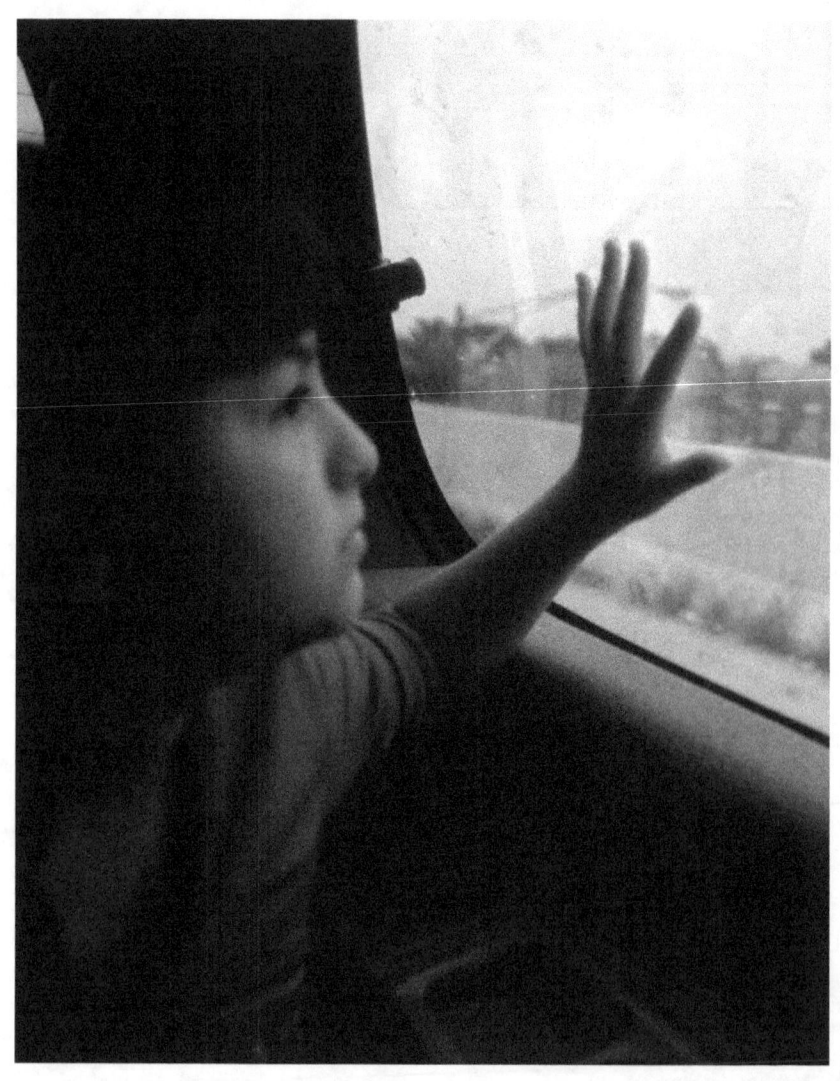

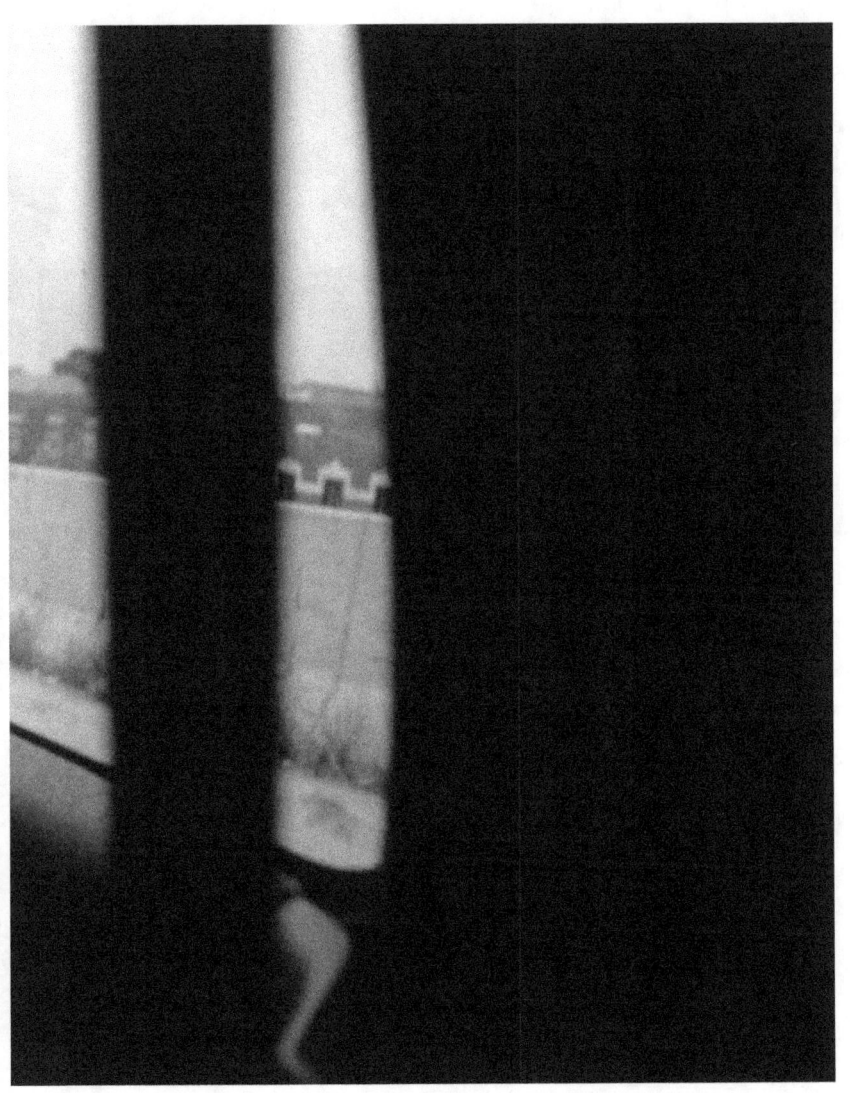

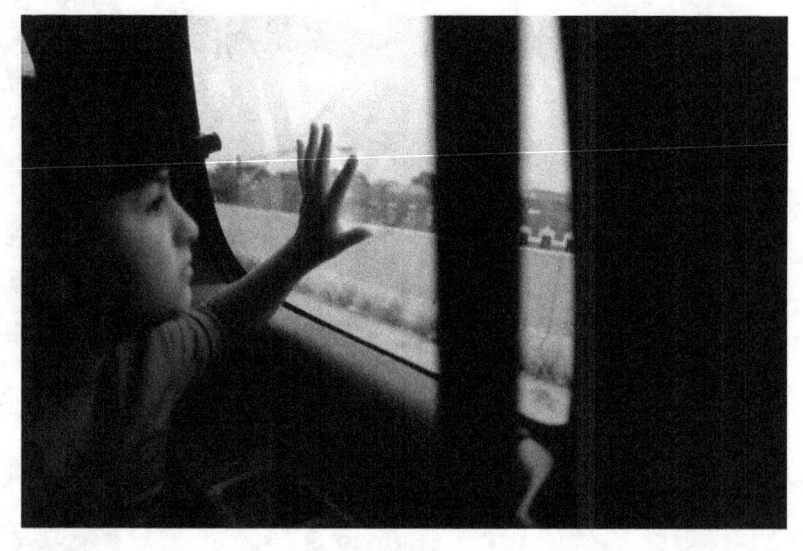

# "Weary Window"

# Illinois

# Autumn

# 2005

# "Ruof"
# 04252006

## The Seasons

utopia world
warm heart passage trough mind cold
universe has told

## The Elements

the green earth is born
ashes from demons will scorn
ice through wind has torn

## The Shapes

four chambers to some
red swords have yet to become
three black leafs have done

## The Horsemen

world corners will die
eight eyes whisper a goodbye
we have one last sigh

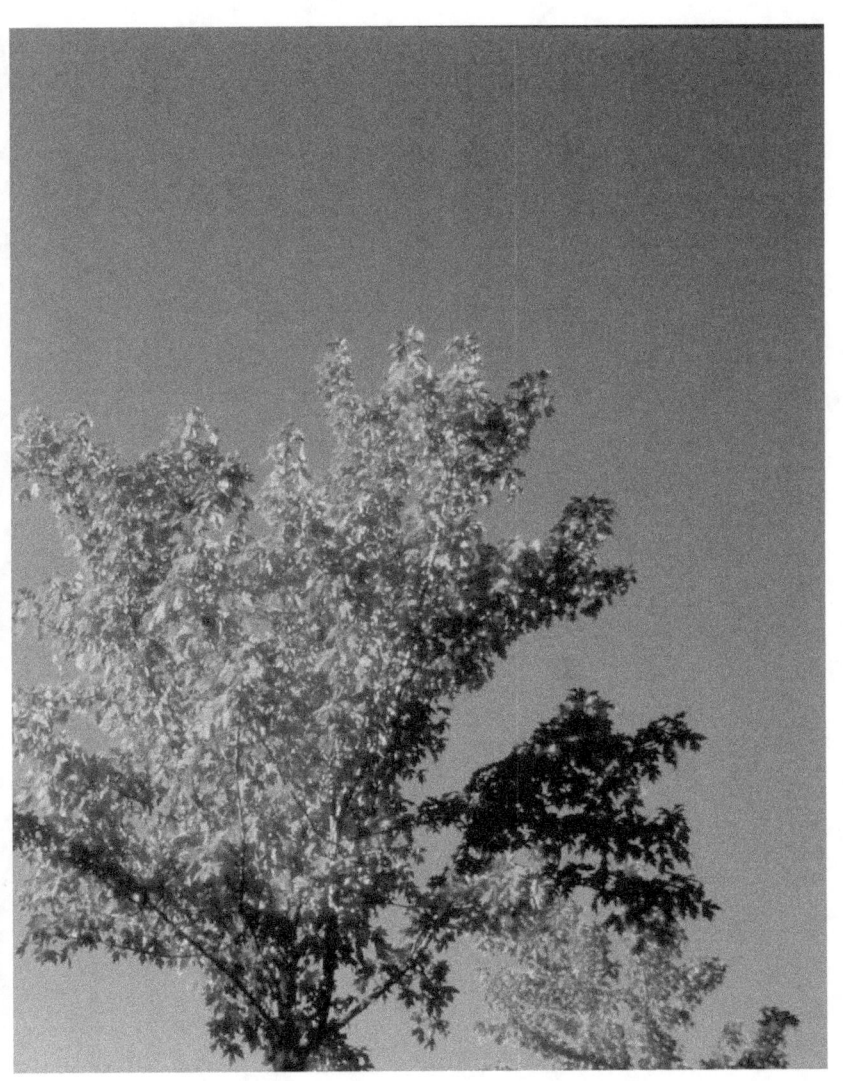

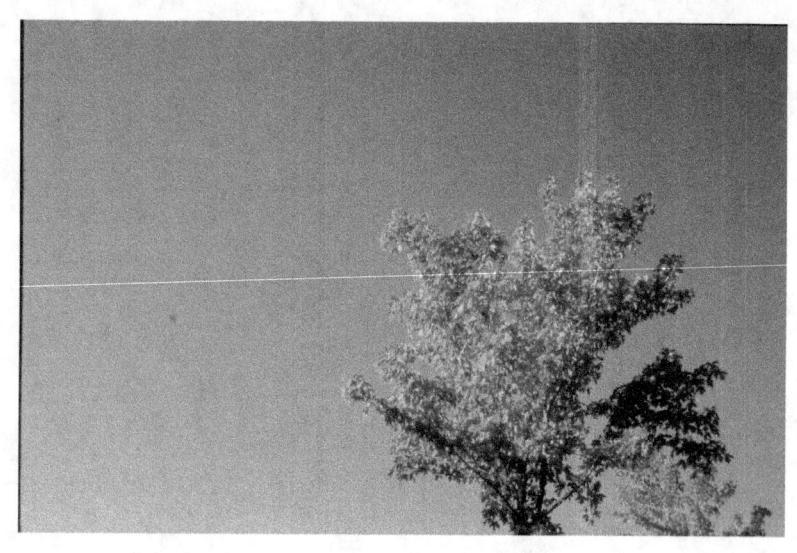

# "Blue Branch"

# Illinois

# Autumn

# 2005

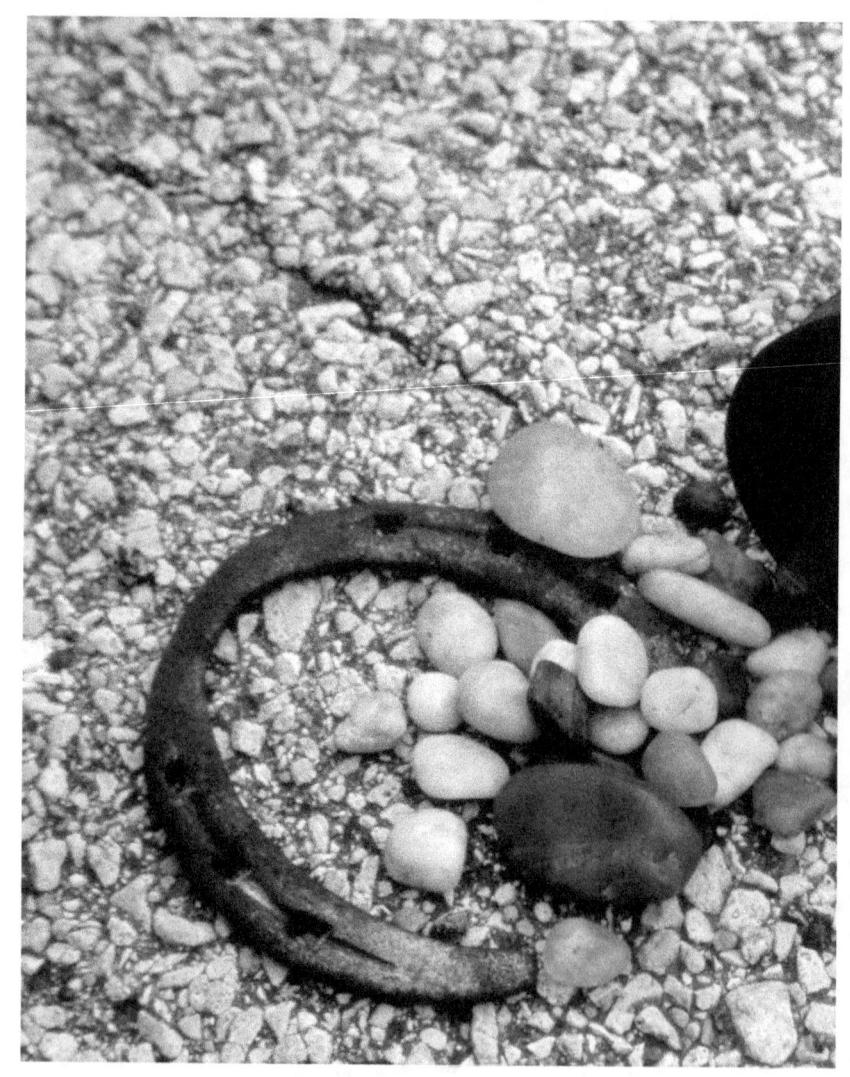

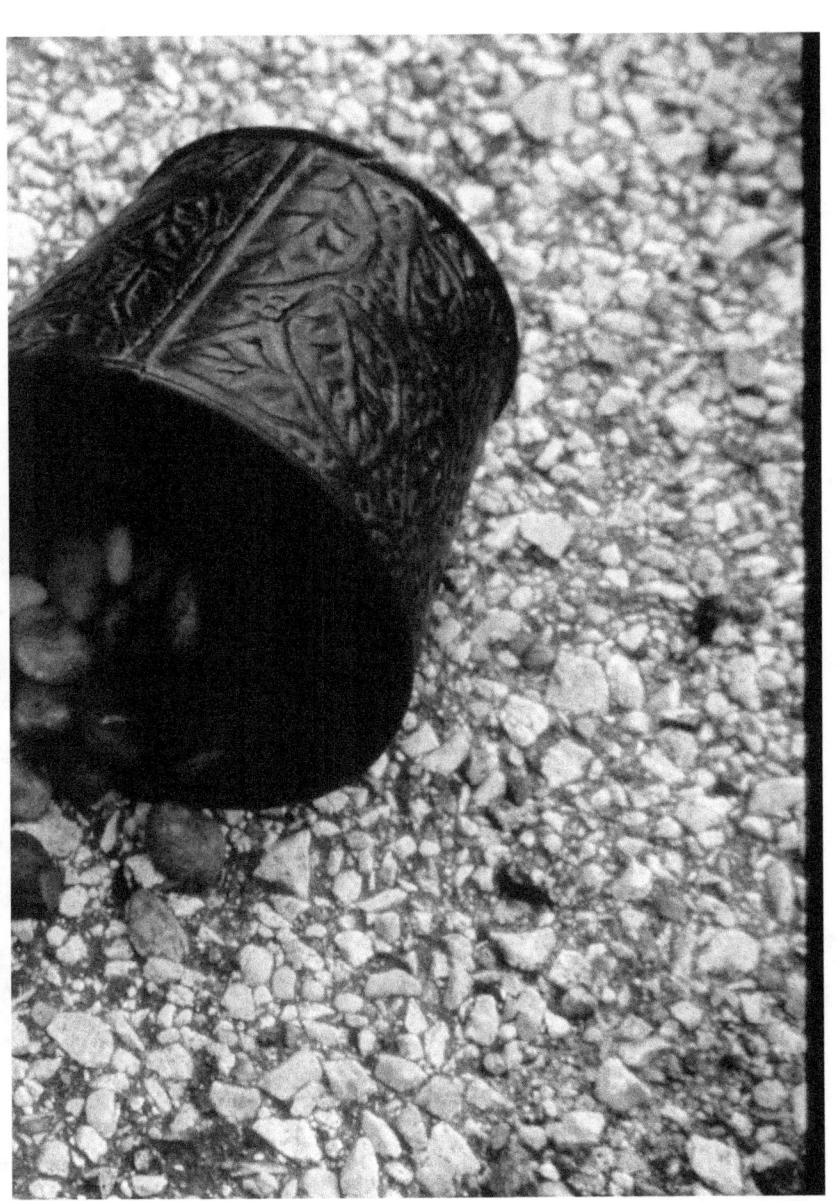

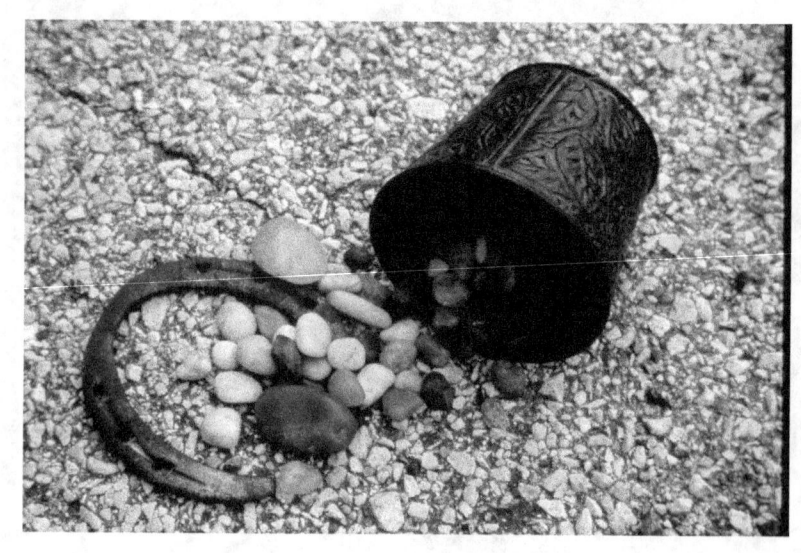

"Lost Luck"

# Illinois
# Autumn
# 2005

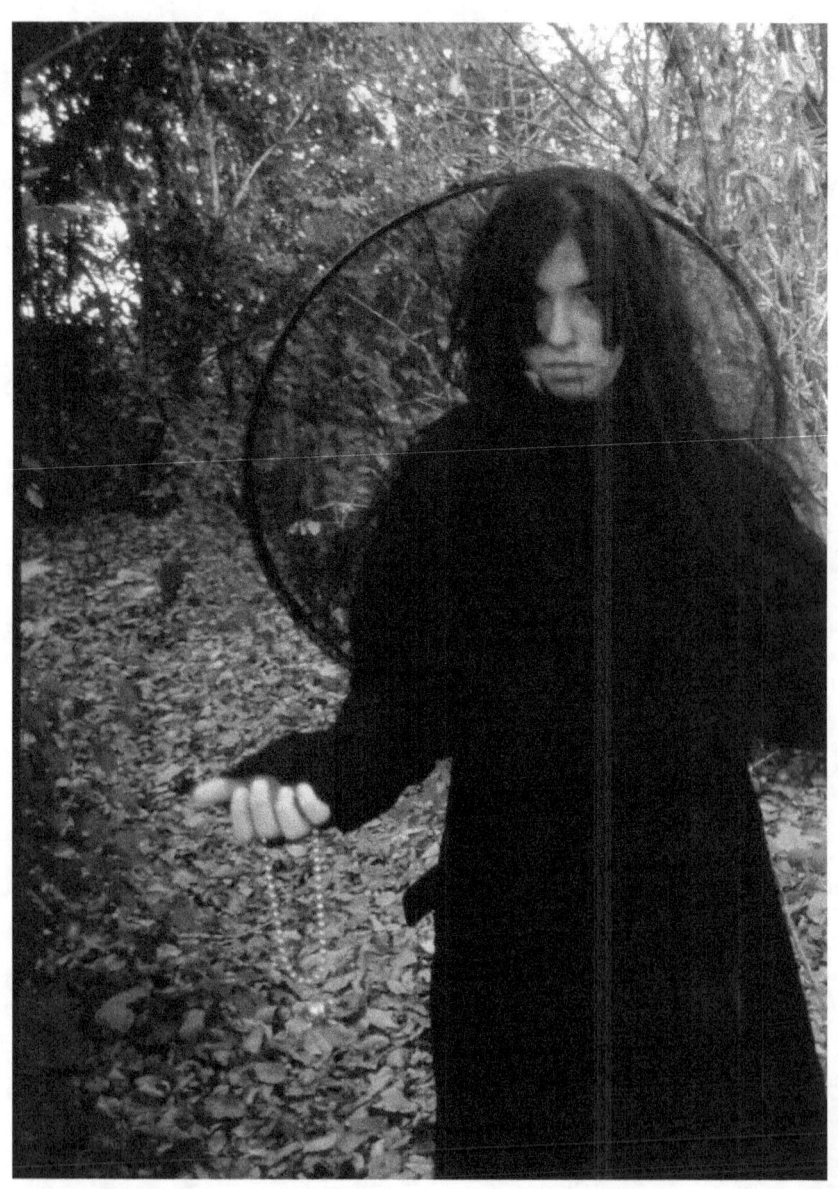

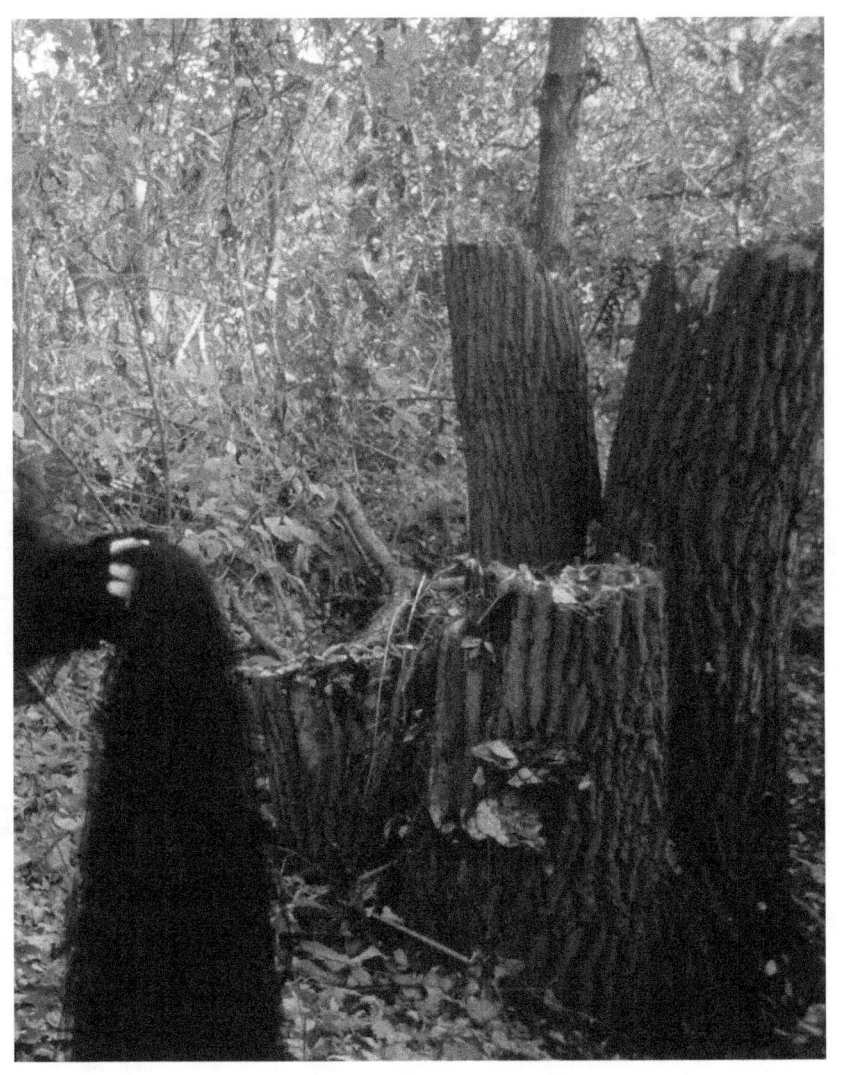

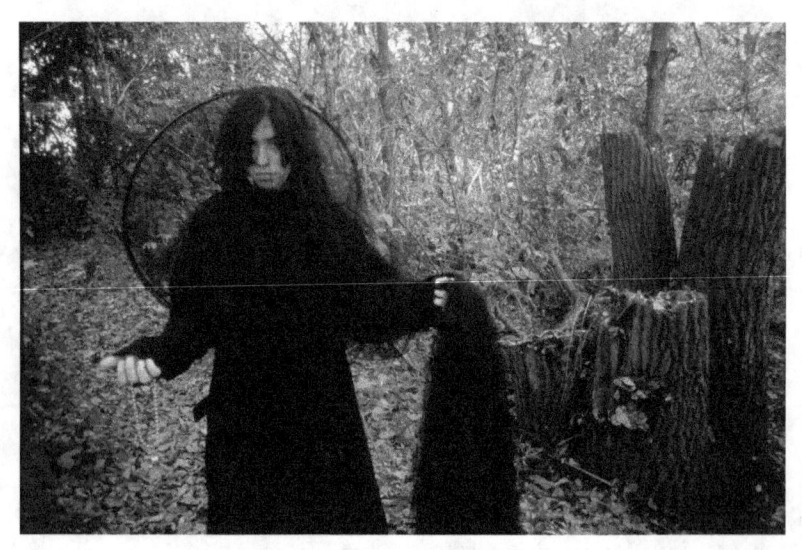

# "Heaven's Halo"

# Illinois

# Autumn

# 2005

# "X Y To The Z"
# 03072008

Not twelve CC's of morphine
Not ten tablets of aspirin
Could stop this gash of words
Two years of spoken pours

Twenty two to twenty three
The same letter to repeat
Like a beat from percussion
Like folly familiar discussion

Exes to the wyes
Perplexes in tongue ties
A B C minuses to be
Two three pluses to form Z

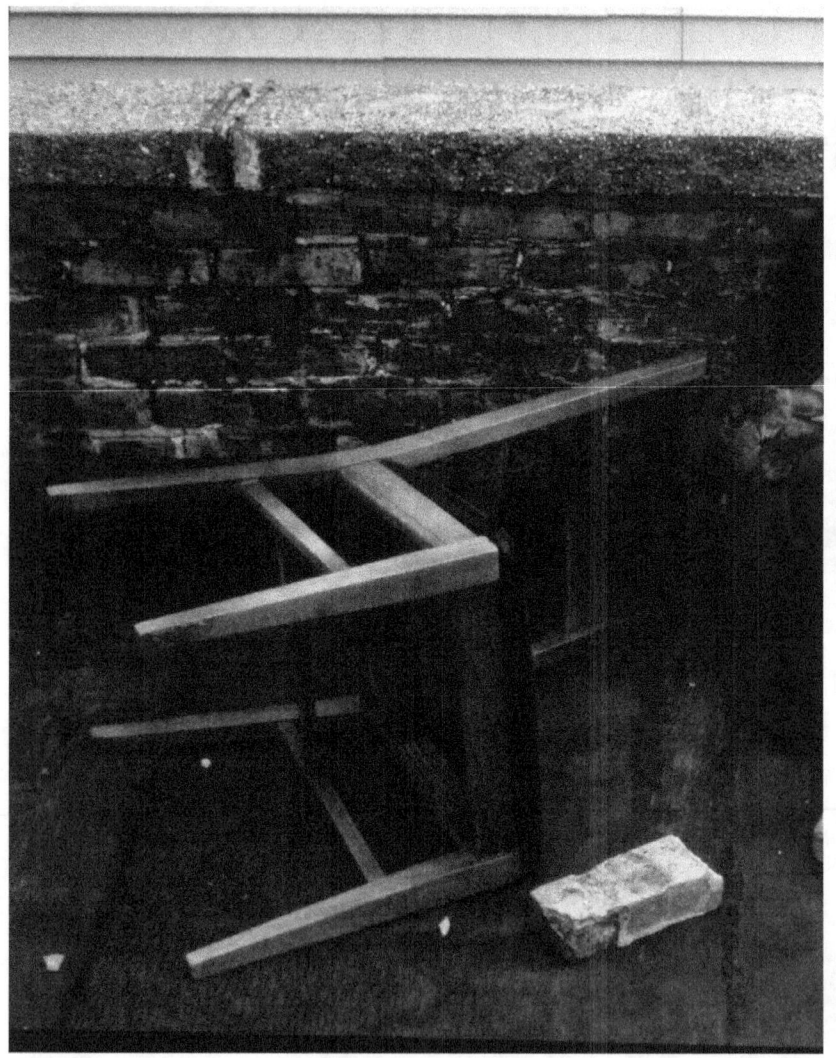

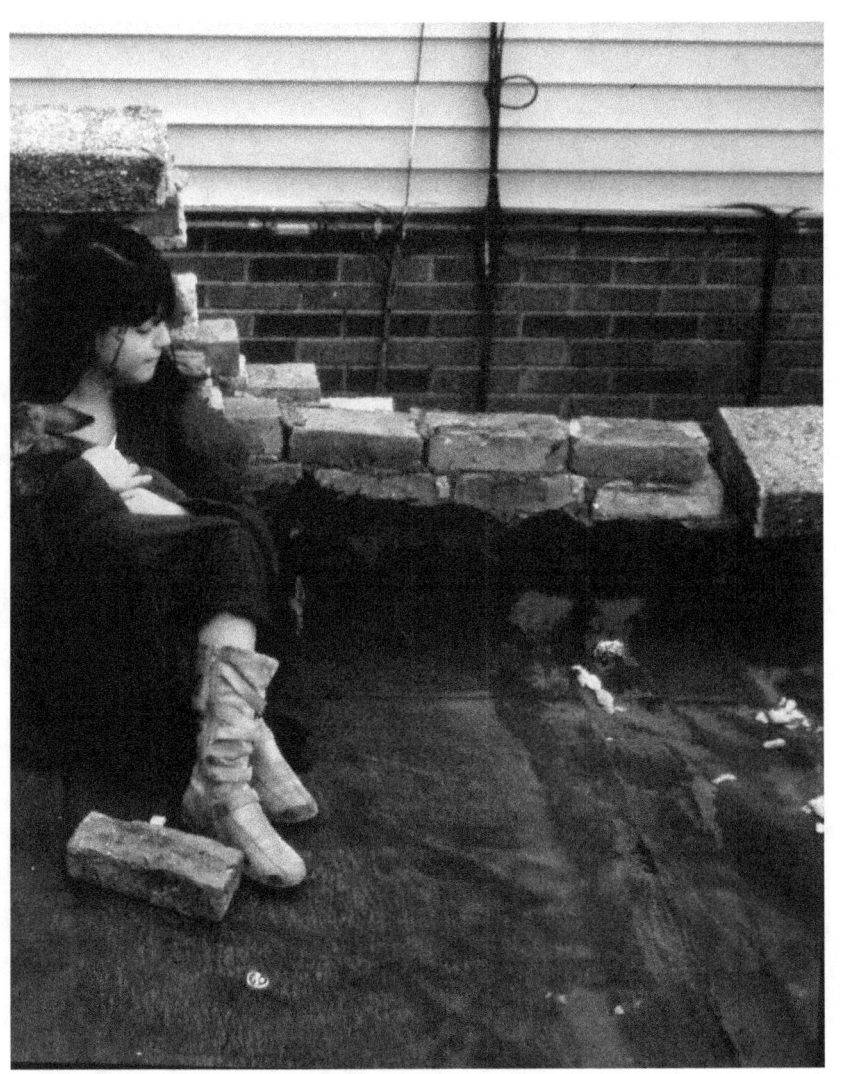

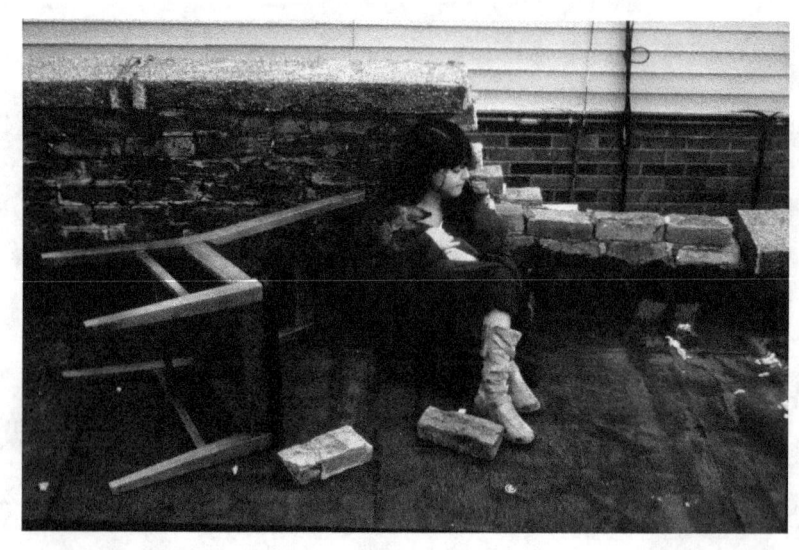

# "Restless Rooftop"

# Illinois

# Autumn

# 2005

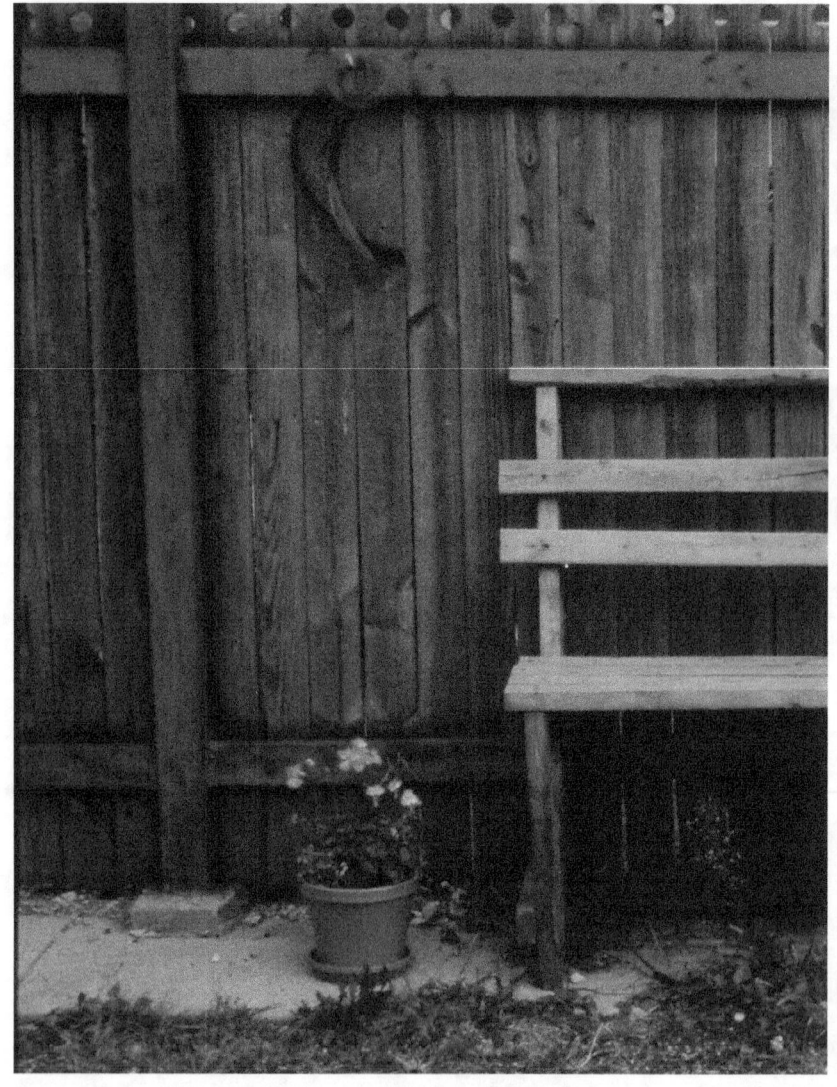

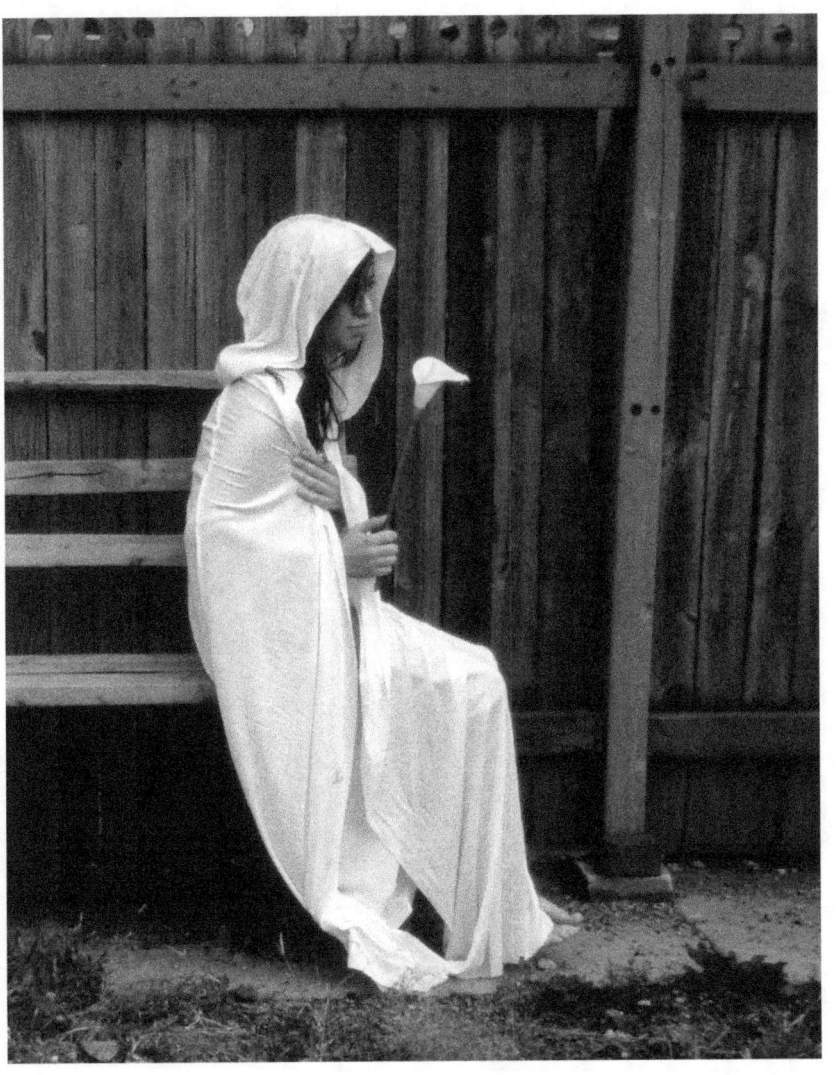

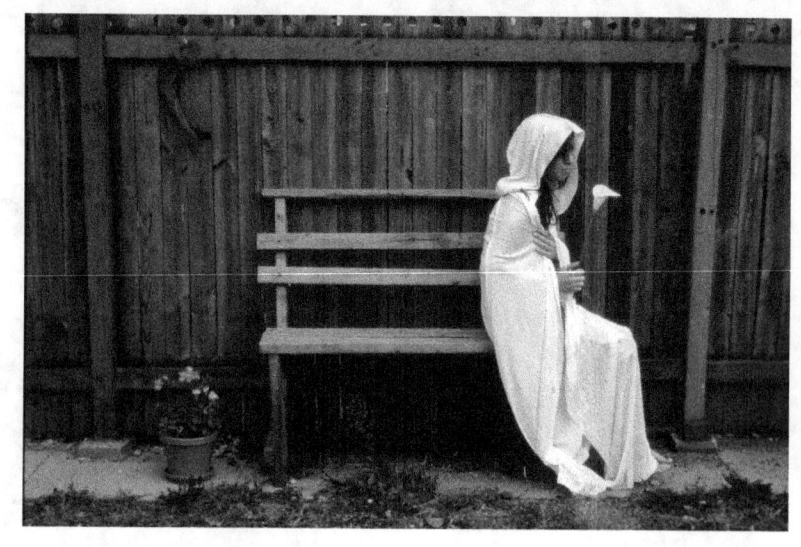

"Lyric Lily"

# Illinois

# Autumn

# 2005

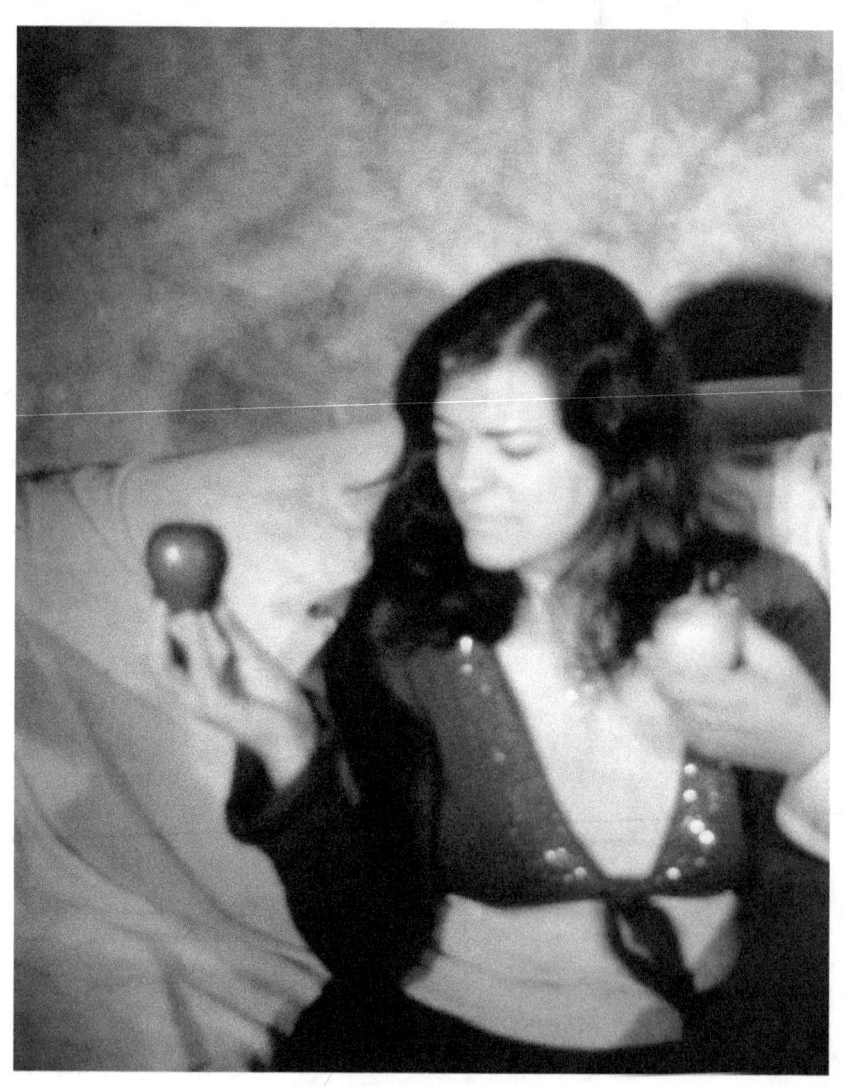

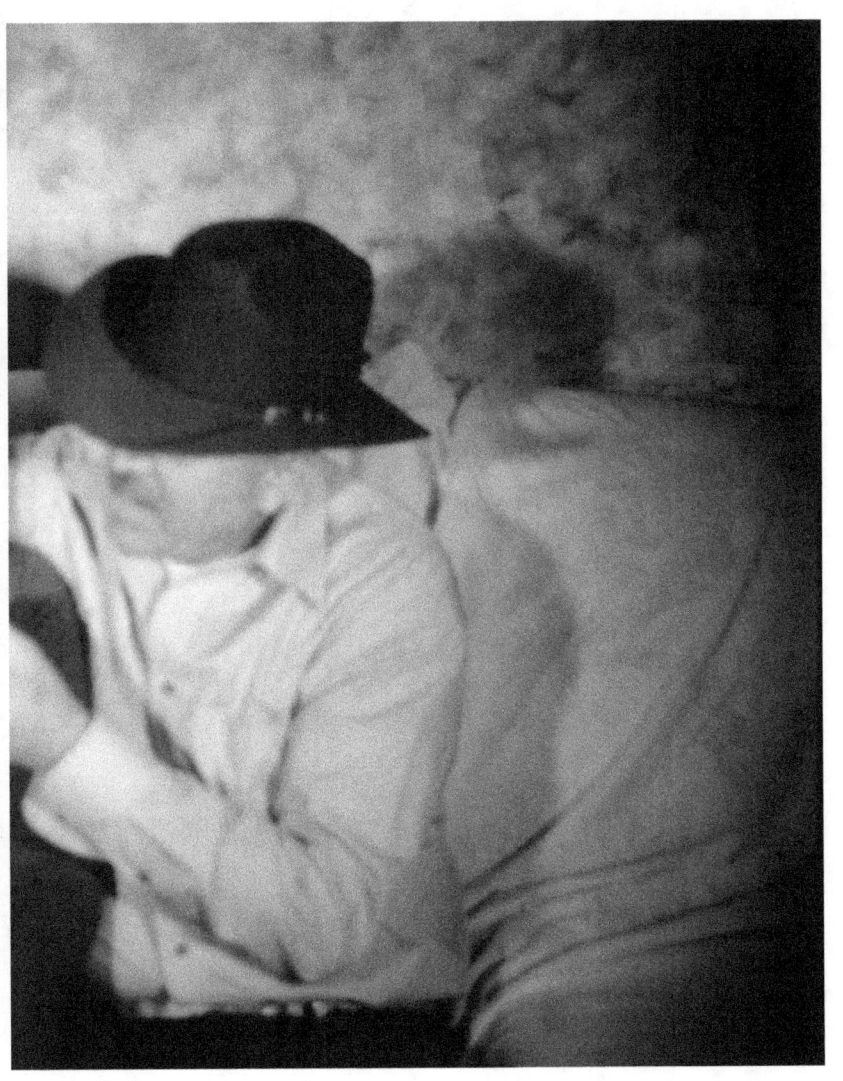

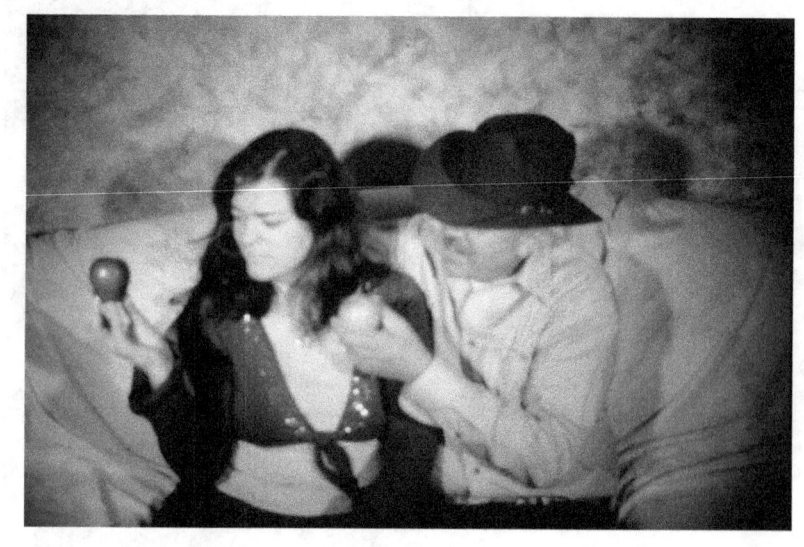

"Dia De Dos"

# Illinois

# Autumn

# 2005

# "Portrait Pensive"
# 03232005

## Part Three: Pisces

specks of eyes akin
brushing a bone form quite thin
strokes of melanin

## Part Two: Capricorn

specks of winding hair
brushing a brunette kind stare
strokes of beauty rare

## Part One: Leo

specks of a short child
brushing a beam fairly wild
strokes of joy so mild

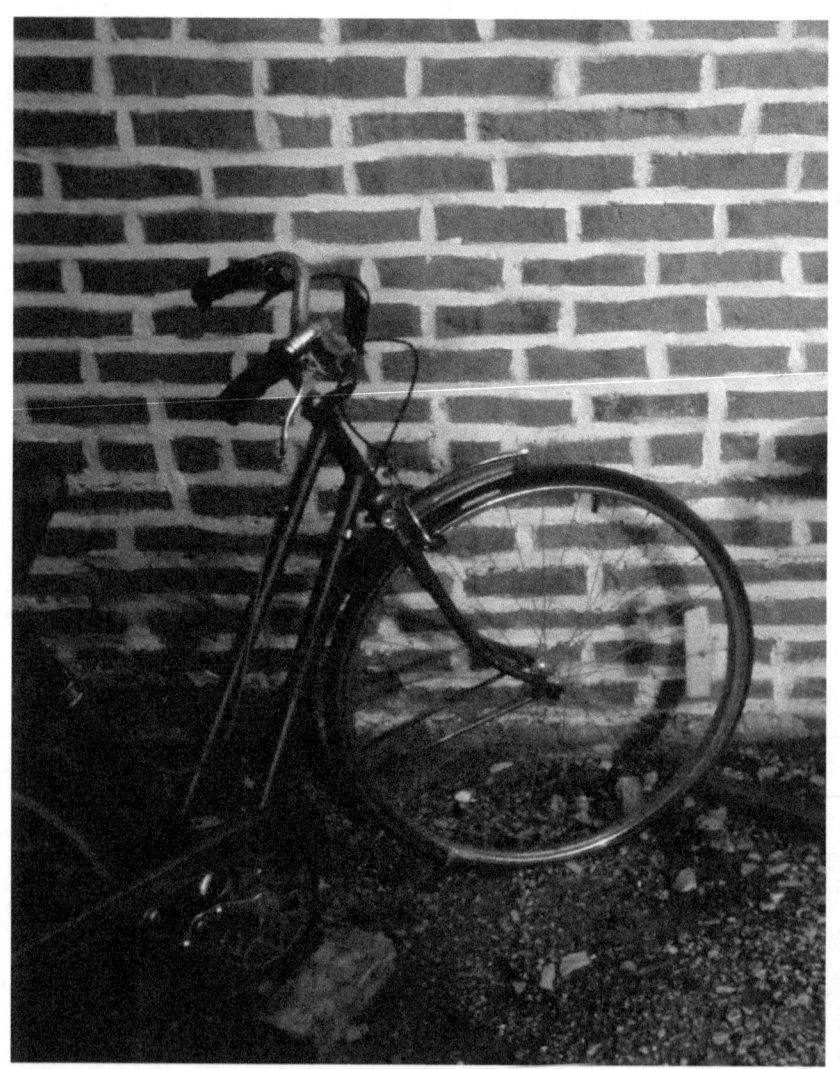

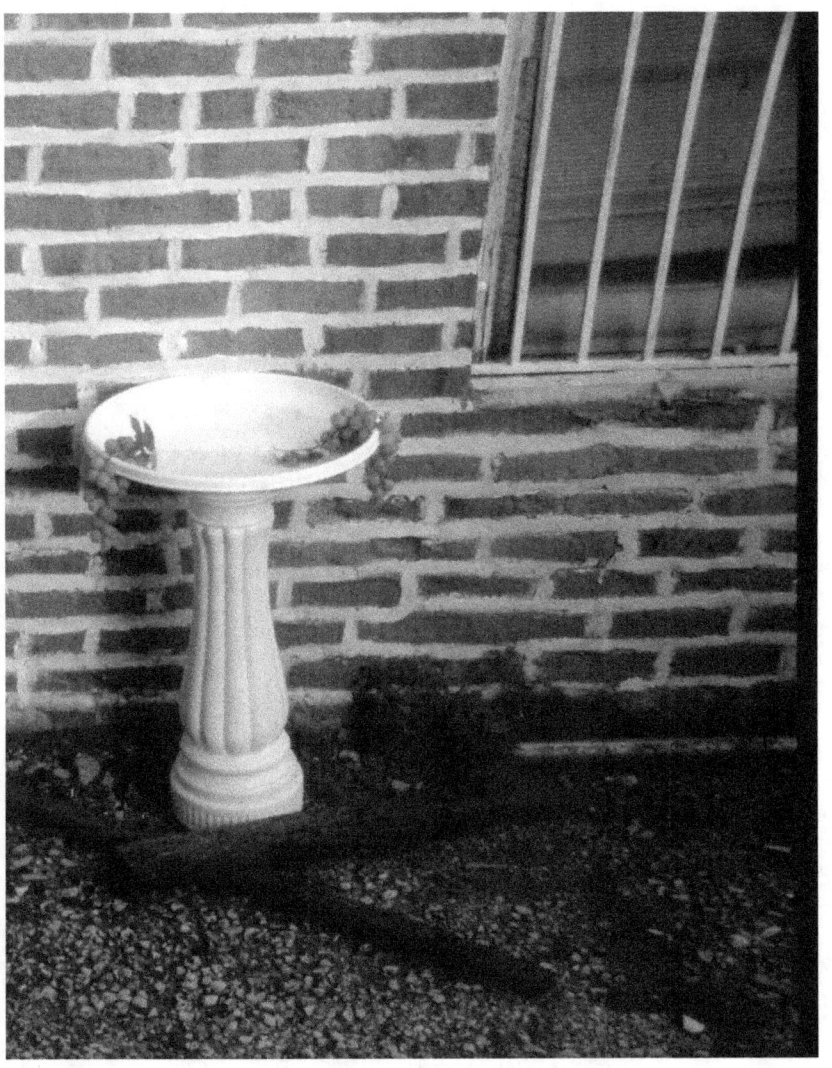

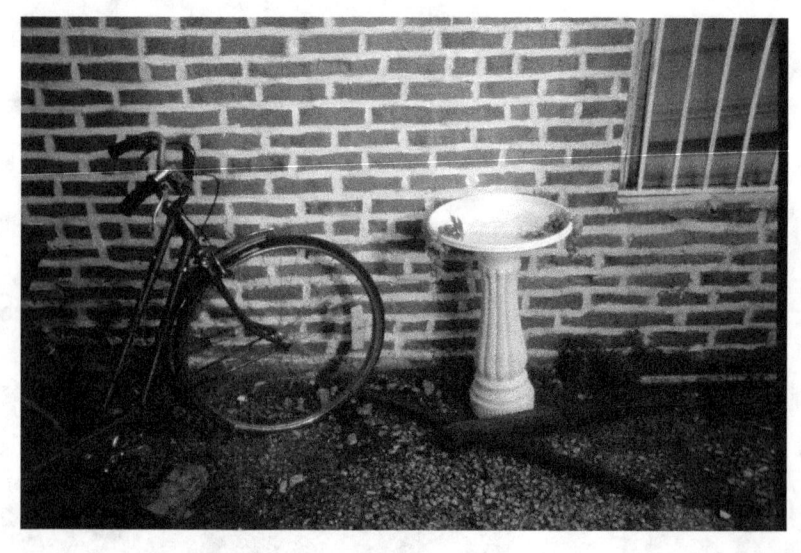

"Bird Bicycle"

# Illinois

# Autumn

# 2005

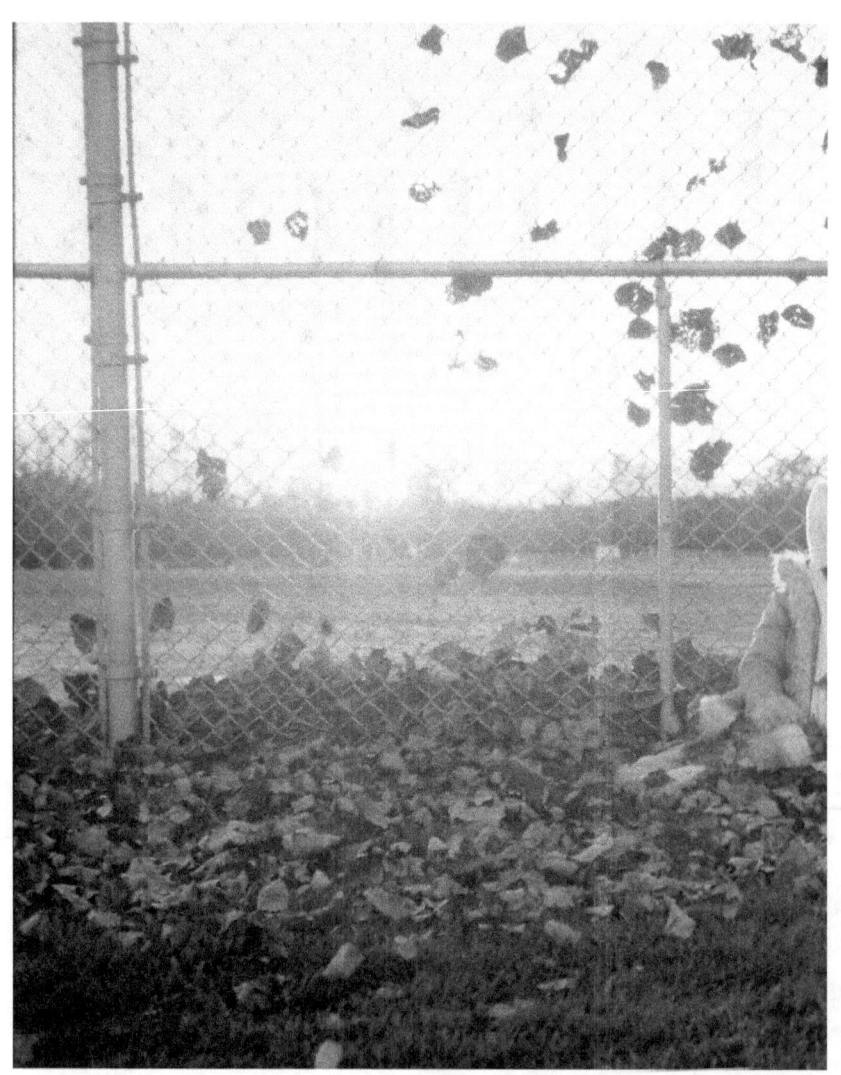

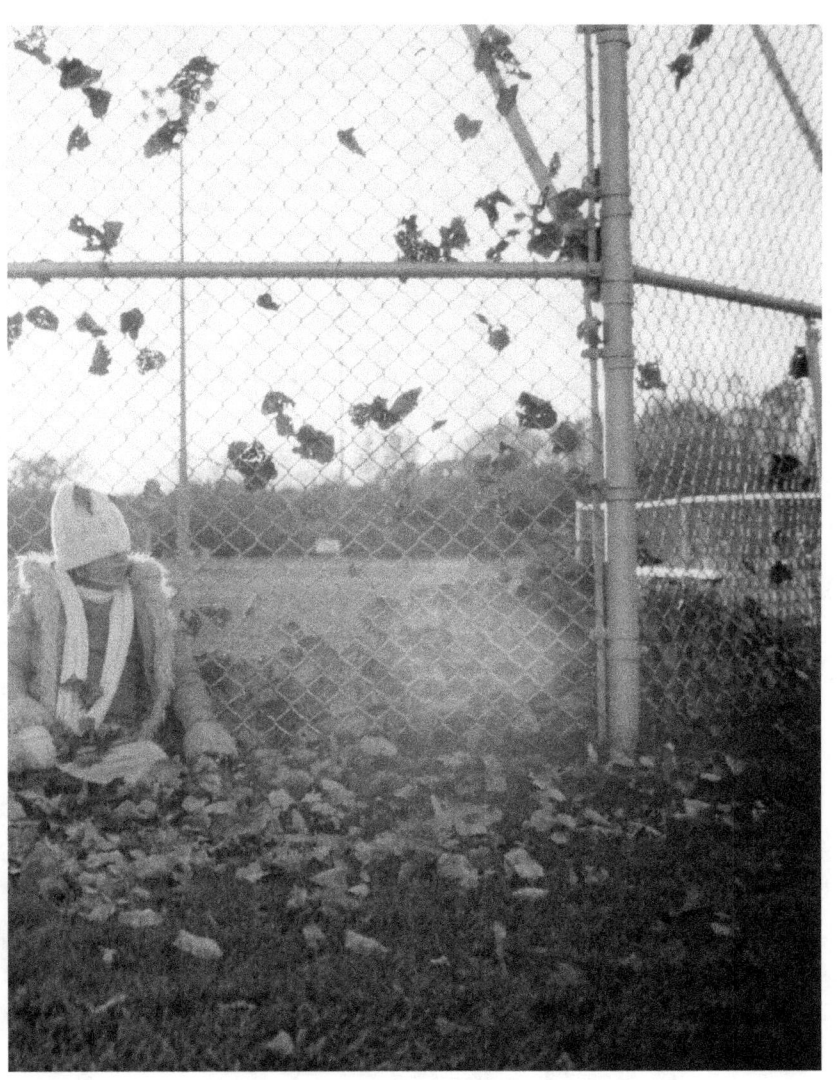

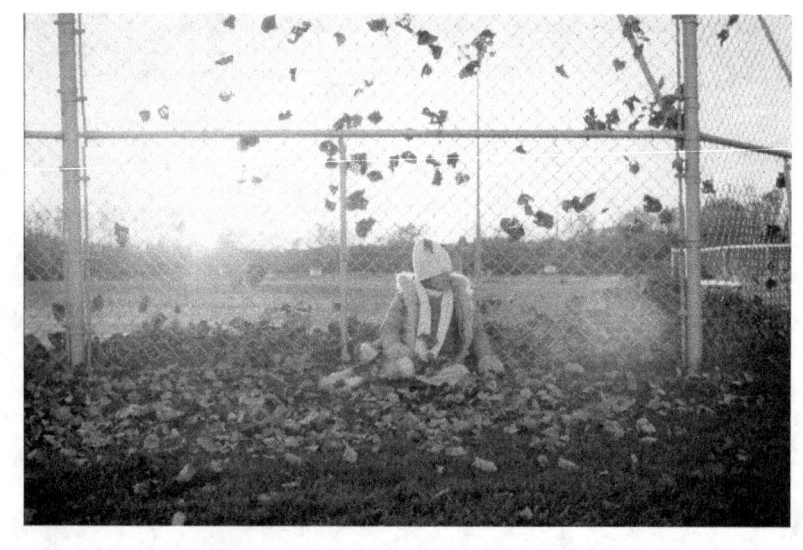

# "Lifted Leaf"

# Illinois

# Autumn

# 2006

# "X Y Equals Z"
# 06162006

A window is being closed

But a door has been opened

A mind is being dosed

But a heart has been broken


This is the part when we begin

This is the entrance where we come in

This is the volume that we produce

This is the square we fly out through


Here we come ready to

Start a fresh interlude

Now that we are illiterate

Increasing the neurotic rate


It is the turn of the century

It is time to write our story

It is the era to spit out notes

It is the decade to create quotes


Here we come ready to

Start a fresh interlude

Now that we are literate

Decreasing the neurotic rate


We paint uncanny calligraphy

We change the meaning of the letter phi

We introduce a new kind of parchment

We have ideas heavier than cement


Here we come ready to

Start a fresh interlude

Now that we have opened the gate

Escalating the spontaneous escalade


This is the part when we begin

This is the entrance where we come in

This is the volume that we produce

This is the square we fly out through

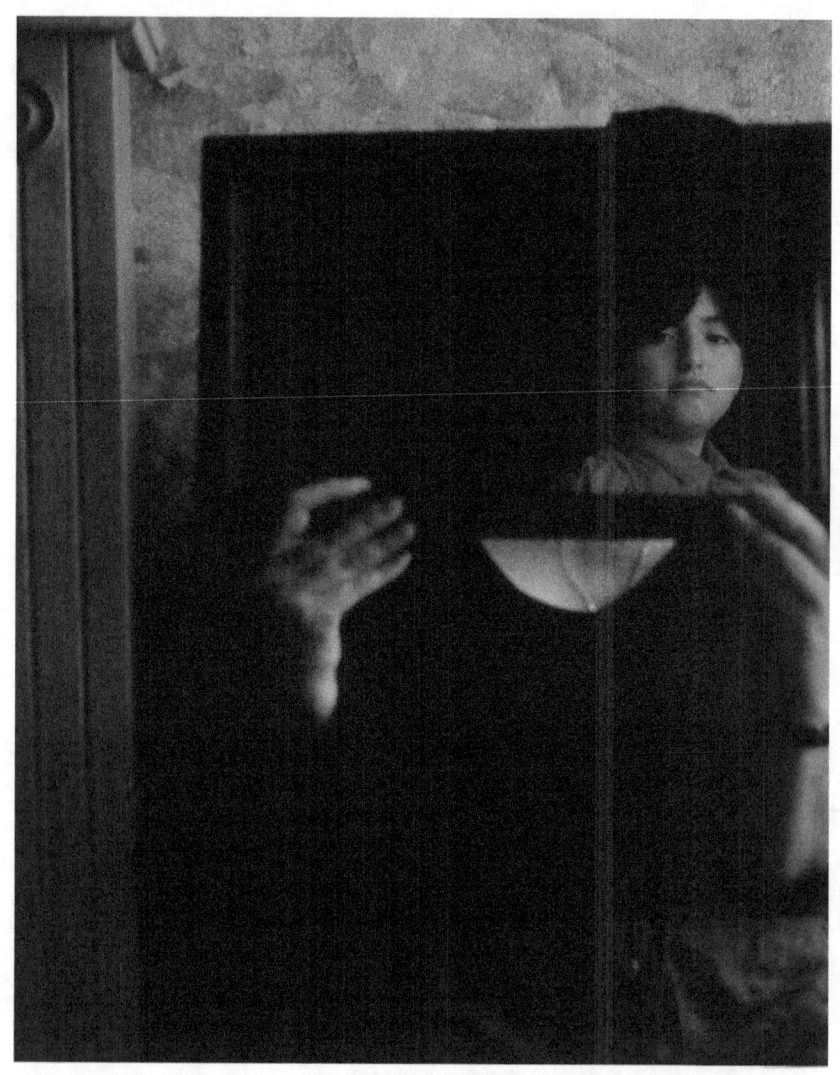

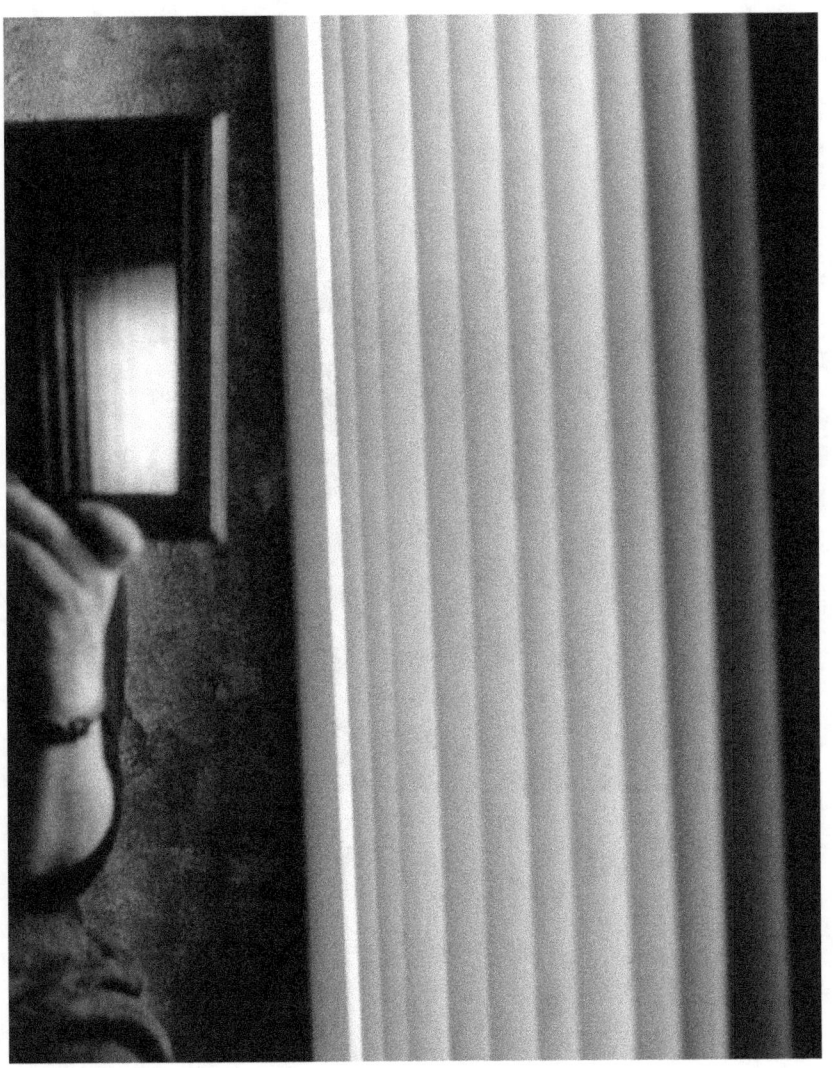

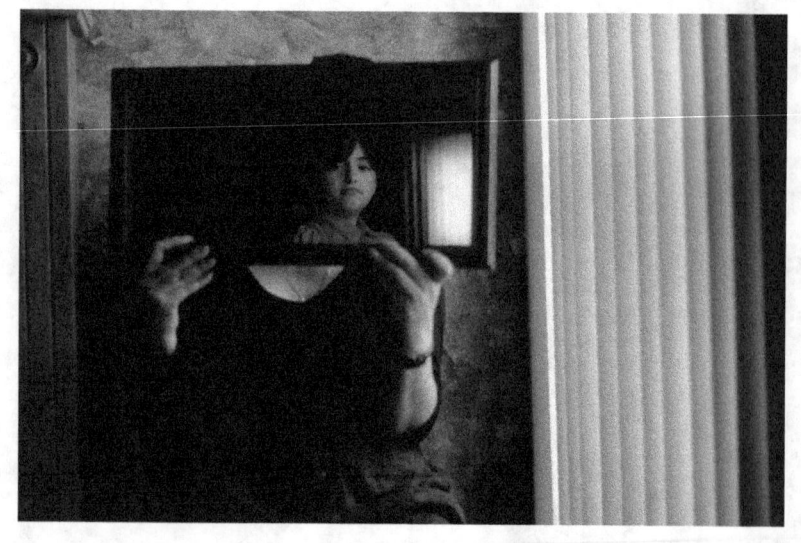

# "Mirror Mine"

# Illinois

# Autumn

# 2006

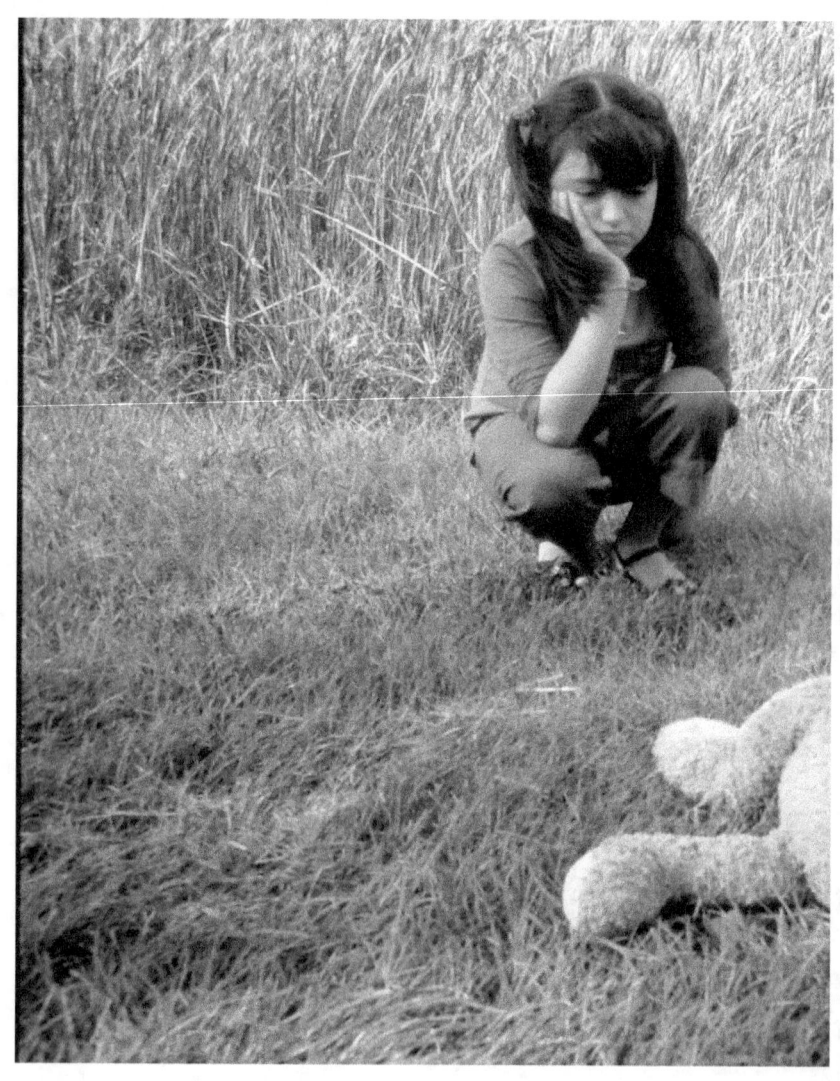

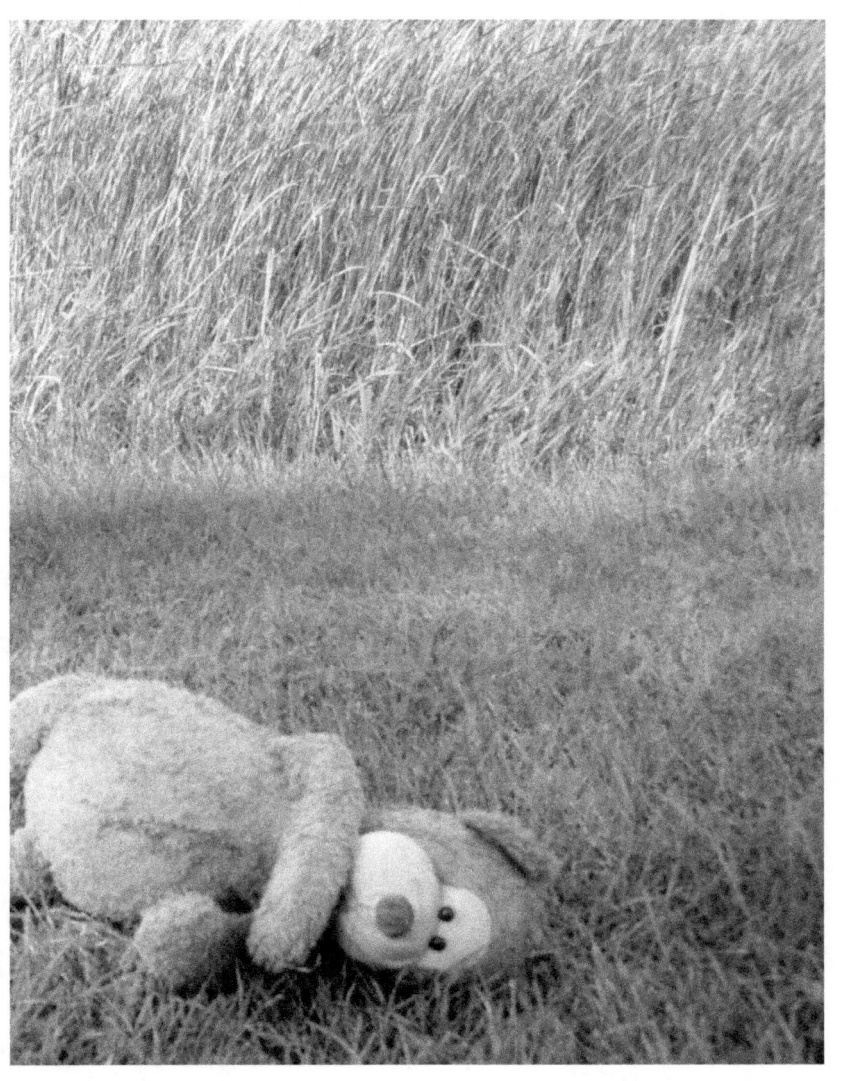

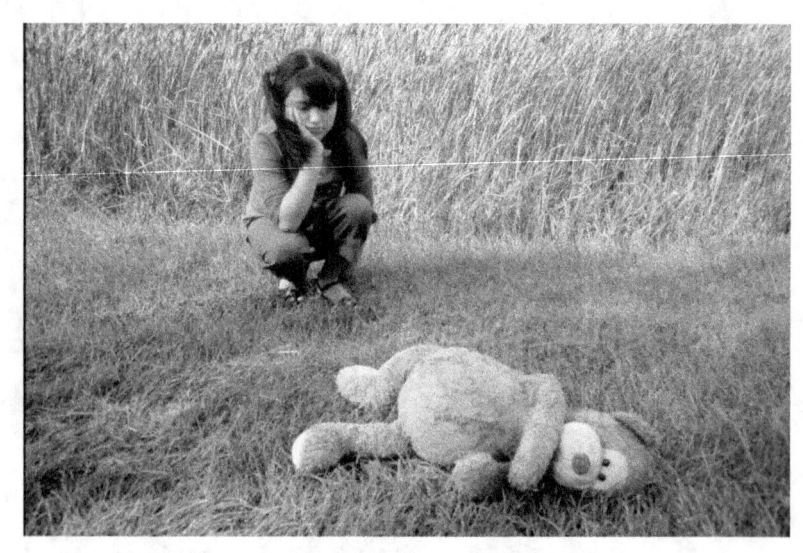

# "An Abandon"

# Illinois

# Summer

# 2005

# "Intermissio"
# 11032006

Crystal lives begin
Sundry hues of soul and skin
Fuse the line so thin


A mind former born
A tear provokes foreseen mourn
A spirit thus torn


Time leads forth sky sight
Upon the returning knight
Keep hearts now in flight

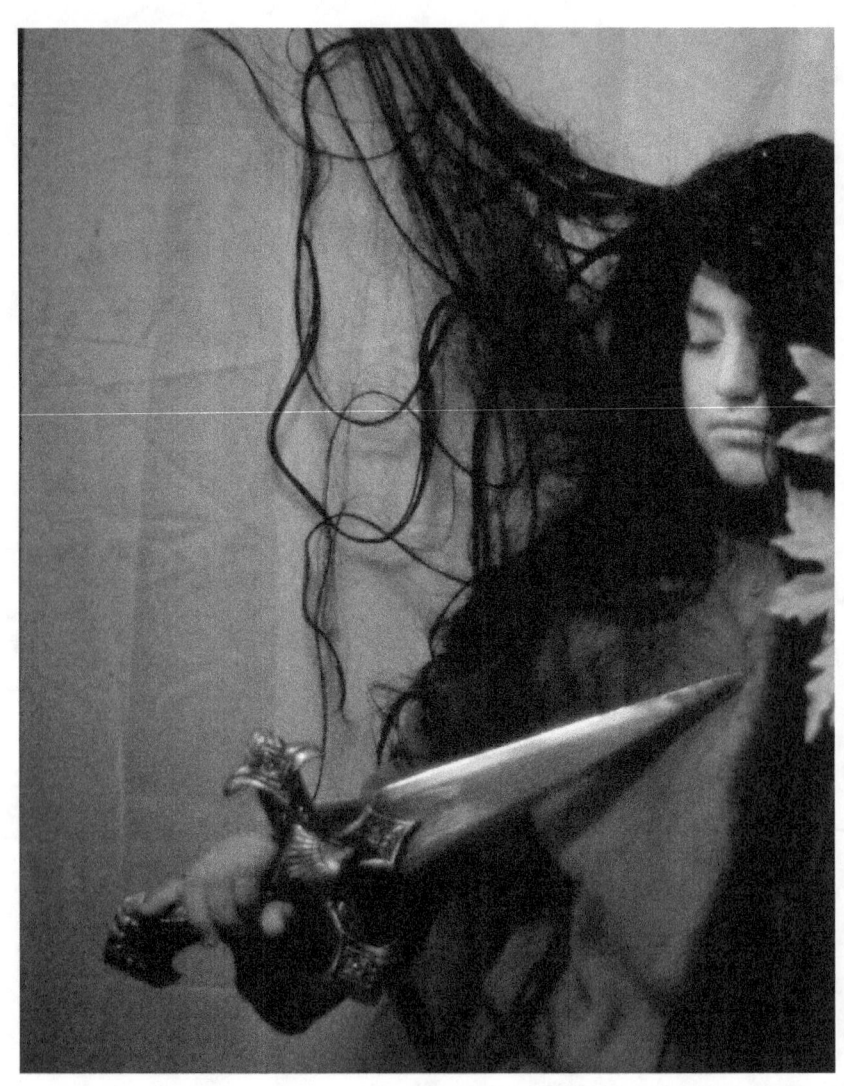

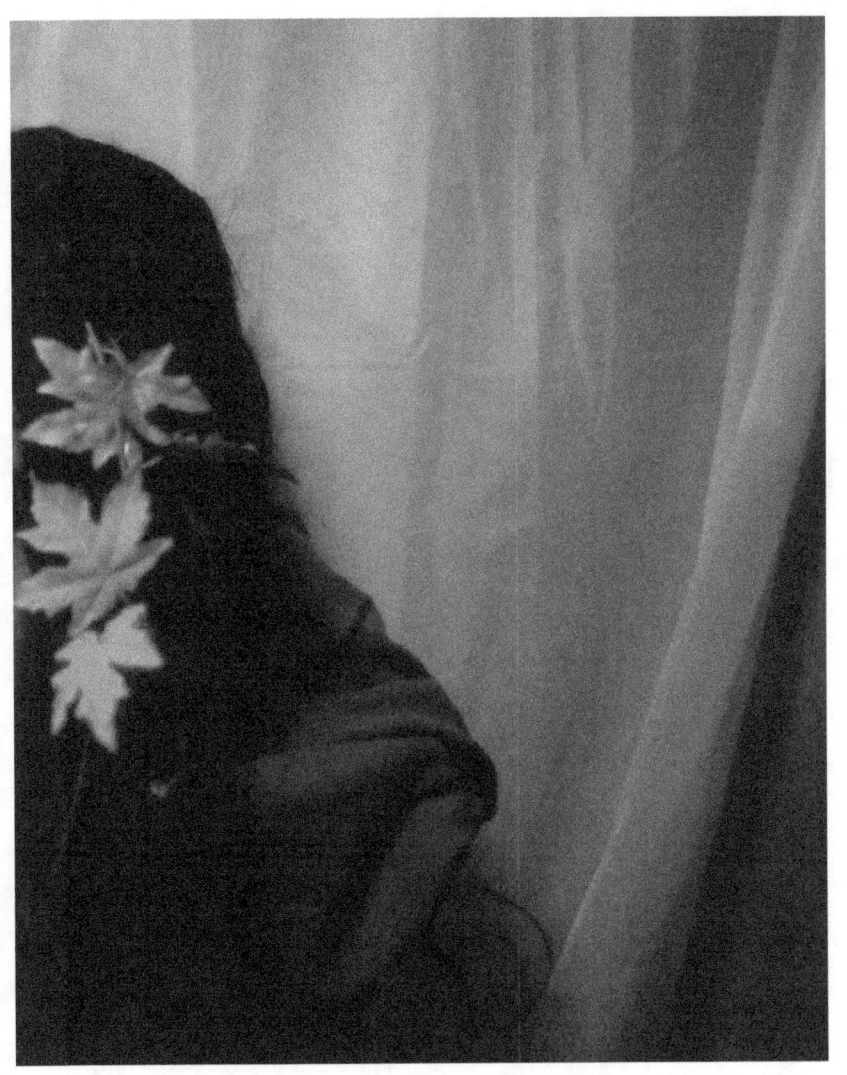

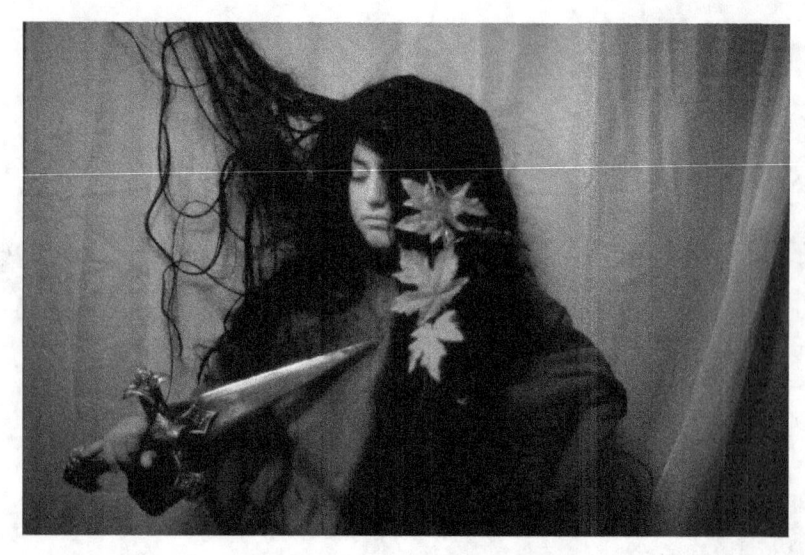

# "Painting Poseur"

# Illinois

# Autumn

# 2006

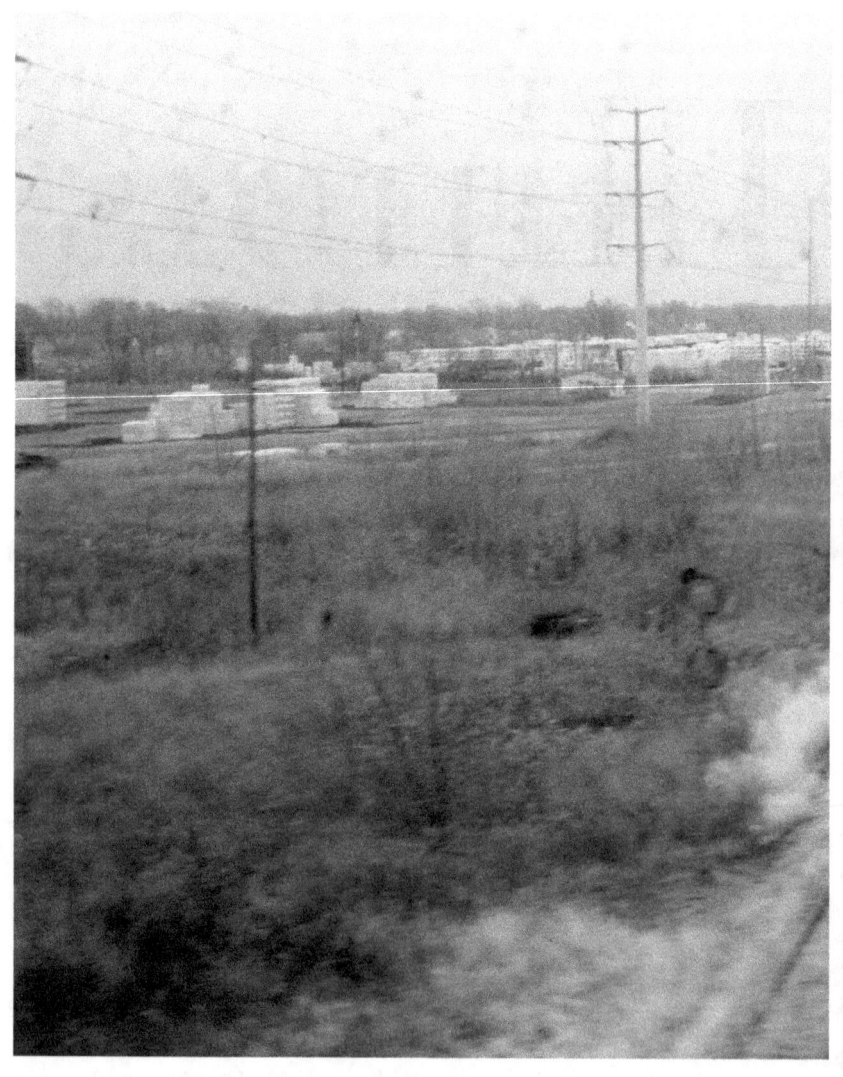

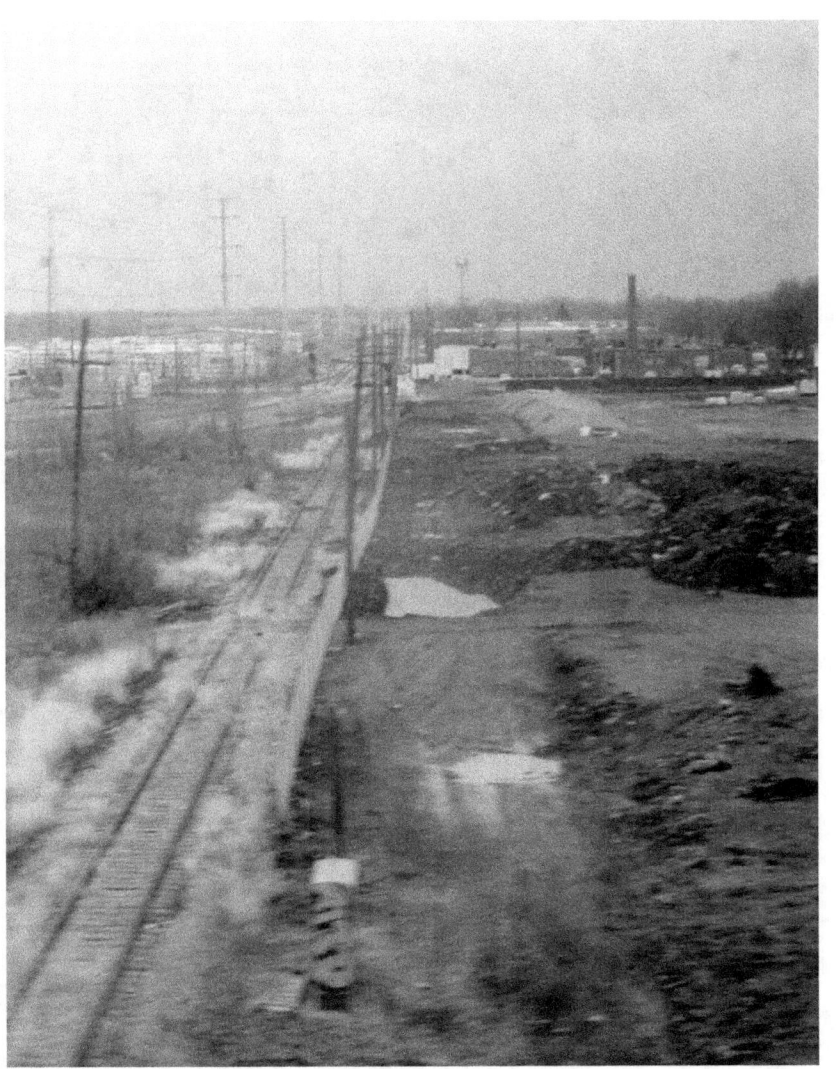

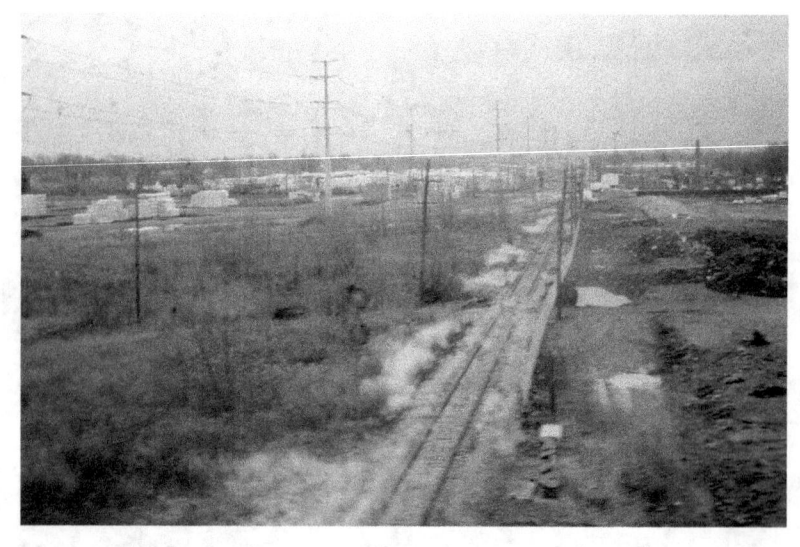

# "The Tracks"

# Illinois

# Autumn

# 2006

# "X Y & Z"
# 08302006

Explaining a rhythm that no body knows
Extending a chord that no one has heard
Expanding two words to make a stand
Exposing a vision through a band

Yearning for a new kind of unheard sound
Yielding the stanzas by the heavy pound
Yelling the lyrics into the microphone
Yawning to the creation of a fresh tone

Zooming through the pages of space and time
Zeroing on the number of words to write
Zoning the mind up to procreate art
Zapping the neurons part by part

Explaining the colors when I'm color blind
Extending the escorts of the limited mind
Expanding the volume of a molecule
Exposing society within solitude

Yearning for water in the core of the sun
Yielding not to walk but learn to run
Yelling inside a sunken glass boat
Yawning to the crash as we float

Zooming across vast opportunity
Zeroing beyond the universal unity
Zoning down the balance of nature
Zapping to kill the power of culture

Explaining to solve the unsolved proof
Yearning that the answer fights against truth
Zooming away from the light into the murk
X Y and Z at work

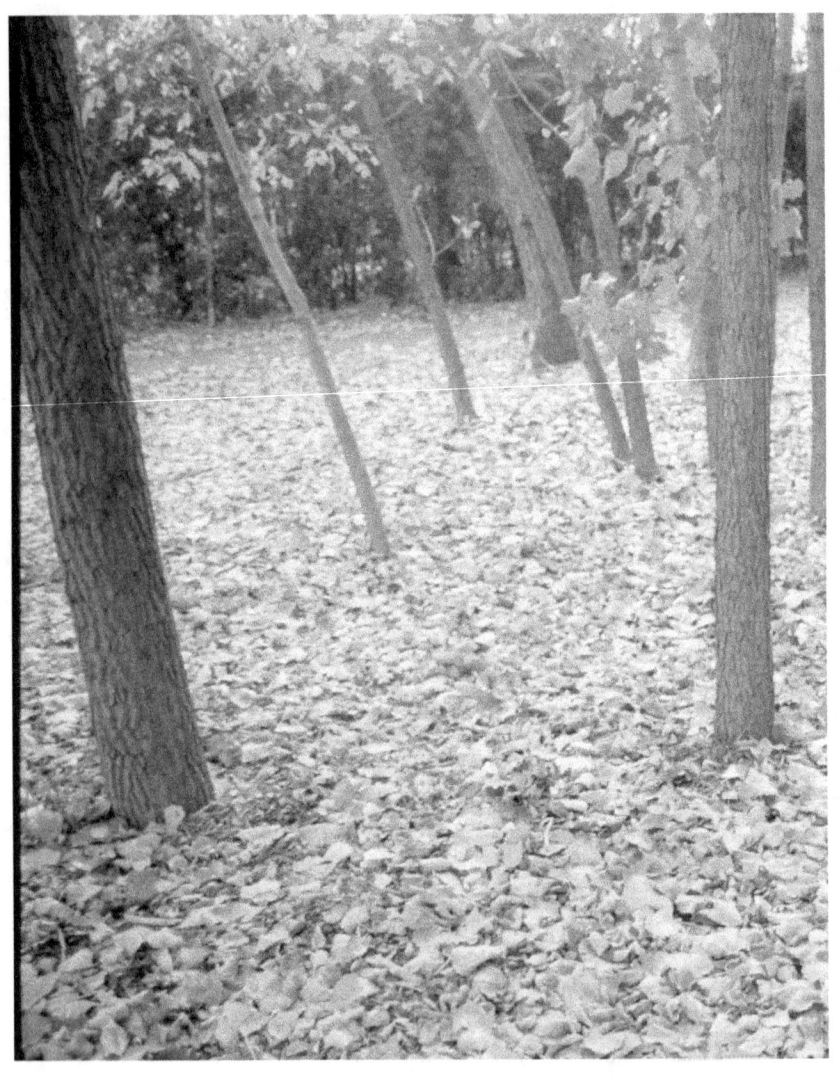

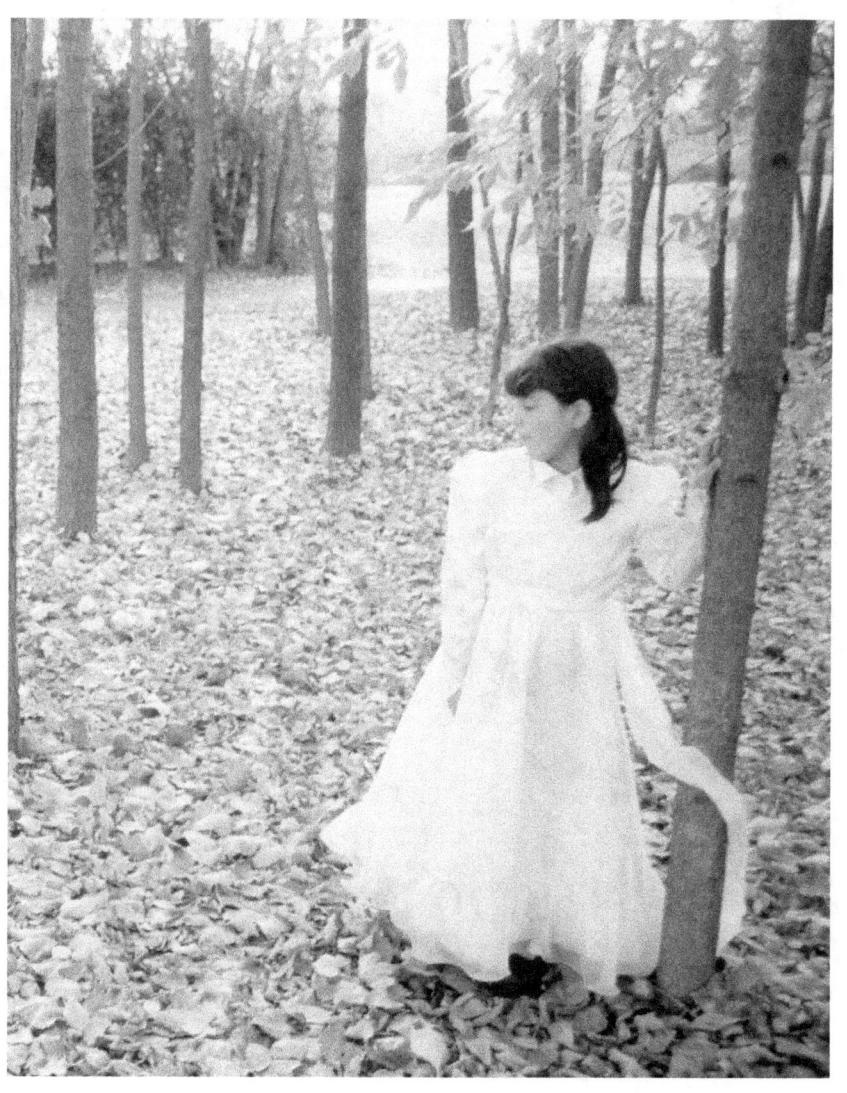

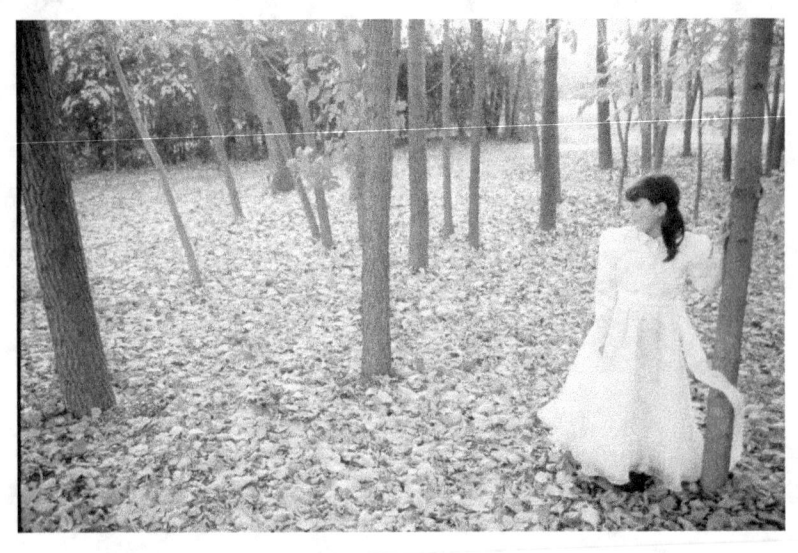

# "Whisper Woods"

# Illinois

# Autumn

# 2005

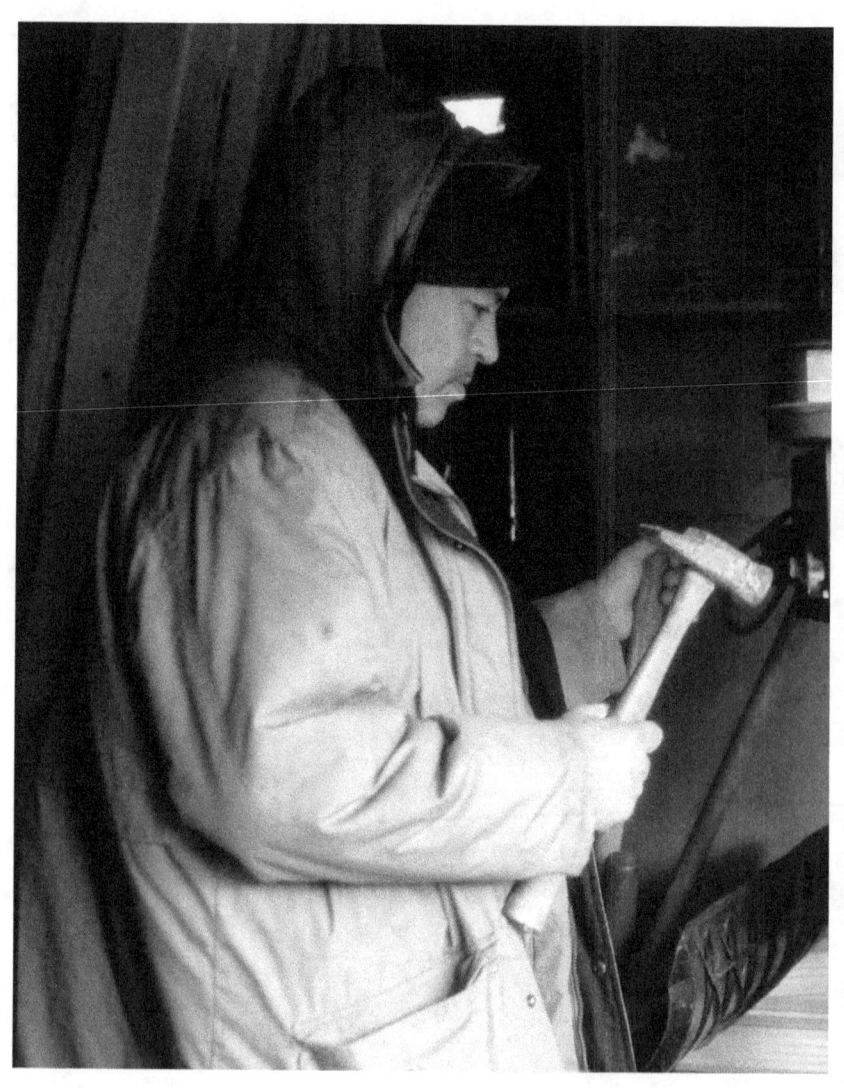

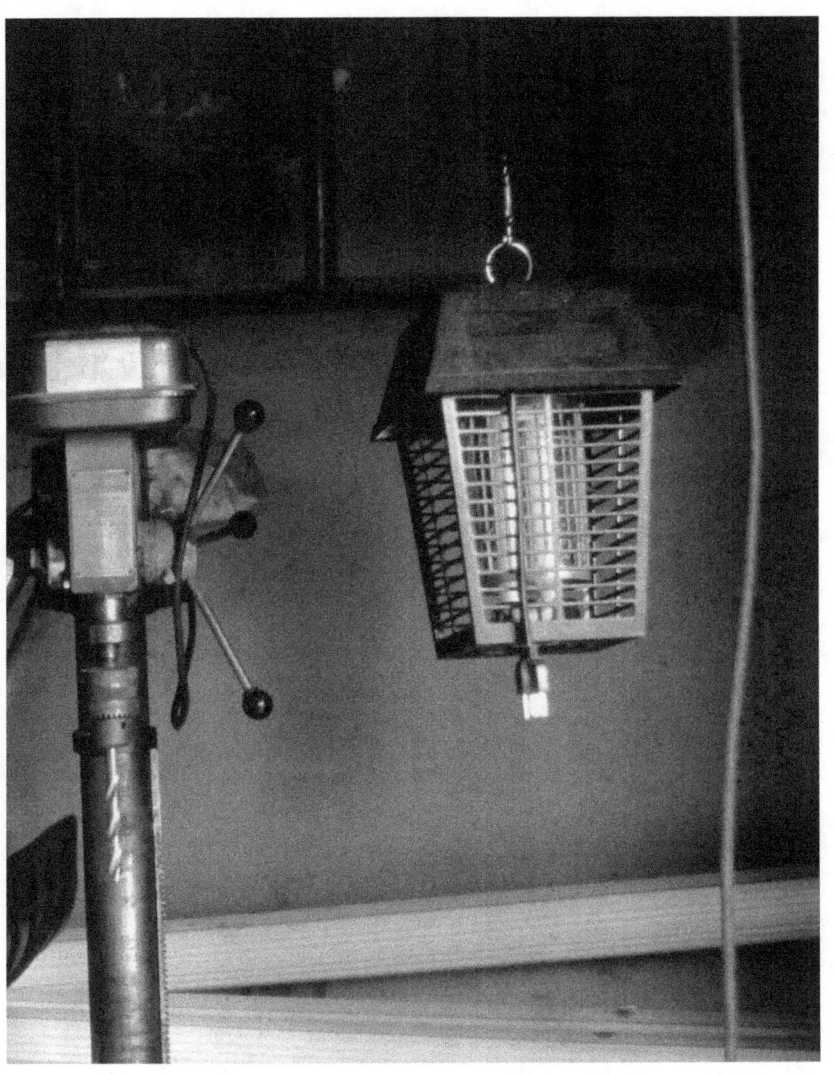

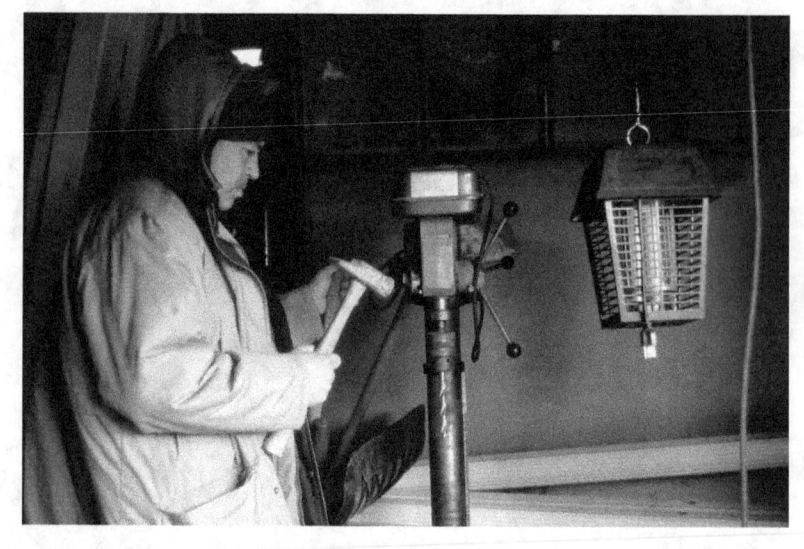

# "Steel Sounds"

# Illinois

# Autumn

# 2005

"These Twentyish Thoughts"

# 09112011

Where have the times taken me
Where do I now stand still
Oh how these feet wish to travel
This infinite world to unravel
Wanderlust runs in these veins
I urge to see an Eiffel tower
When the clock strikes twenty eight
I yearn to read Machu Picchu peaks
Before the dial strikes three too late
Is there a simple reason in a breath
Is a tale being written or fairly read
Why pursue the scholarly paved ways
If there is no payoff in the long run
In itself perhaps yes in itself undeniably
Do diluted eyes fail to see achievement
I forget I forget oh turning skies beyond
Remind me how to appreciate cricket sounds
Give me right to complain just for this round
I am only human and plenty thoughts do pour
Yes yes creativity will flow on scheduled hour
However for now not in land abroad
I must stop the eager questions
I ought to break this self-induced torment
For the days might bring the answers
Indeed the light has always done
My beloved faces and those out of sight
In truth I Am blessed I Am all in one

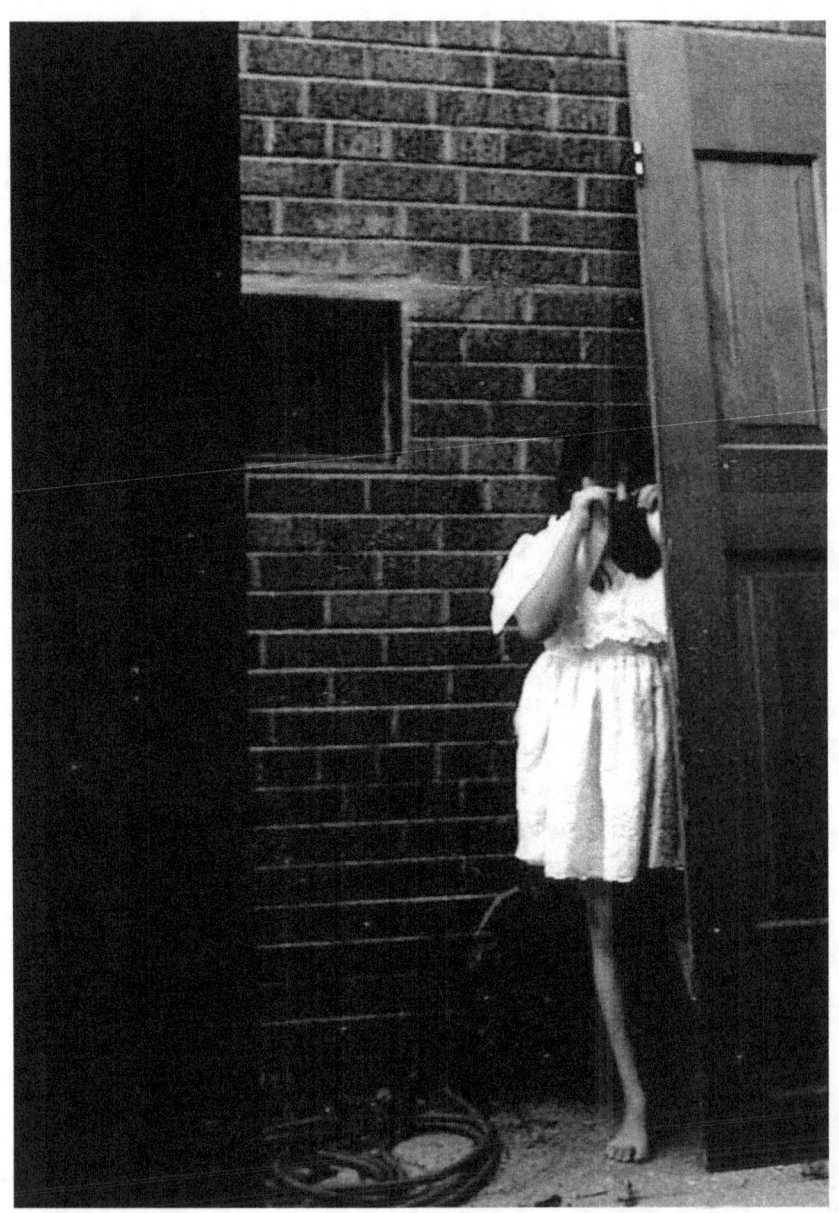

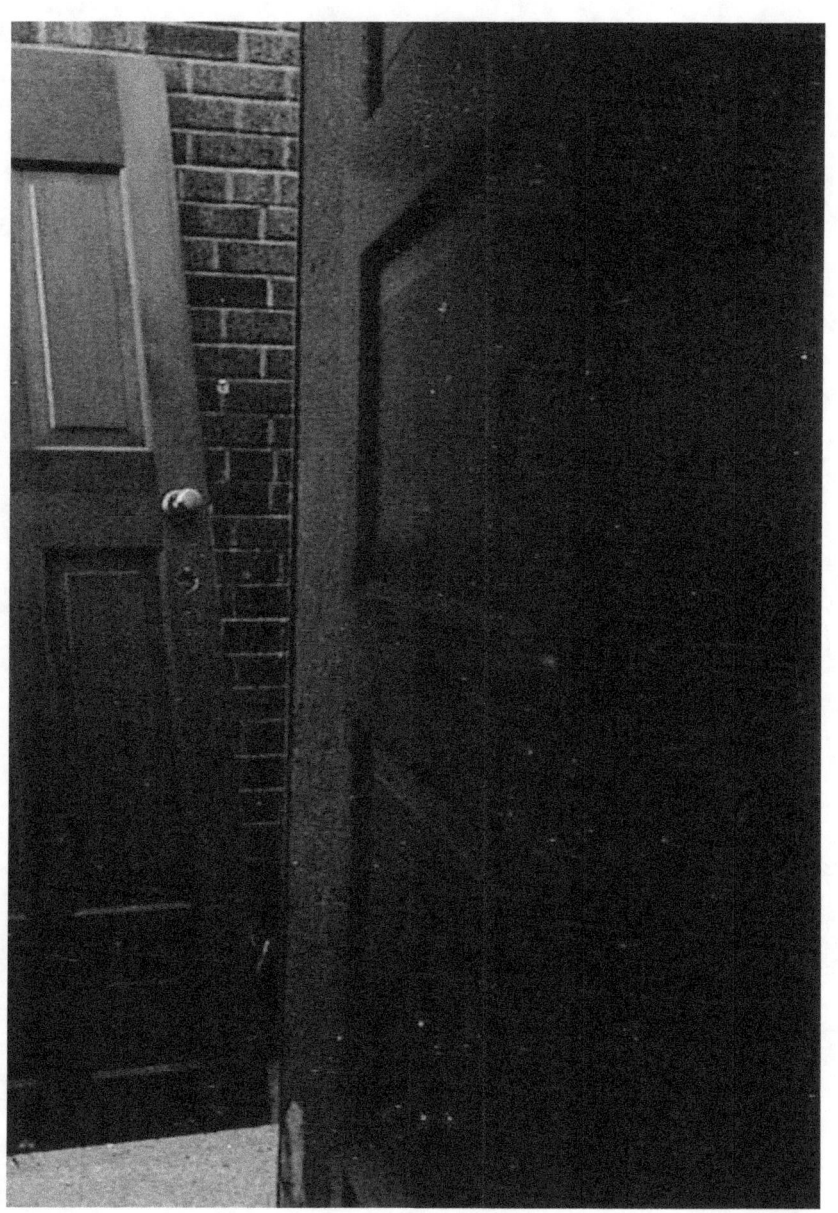

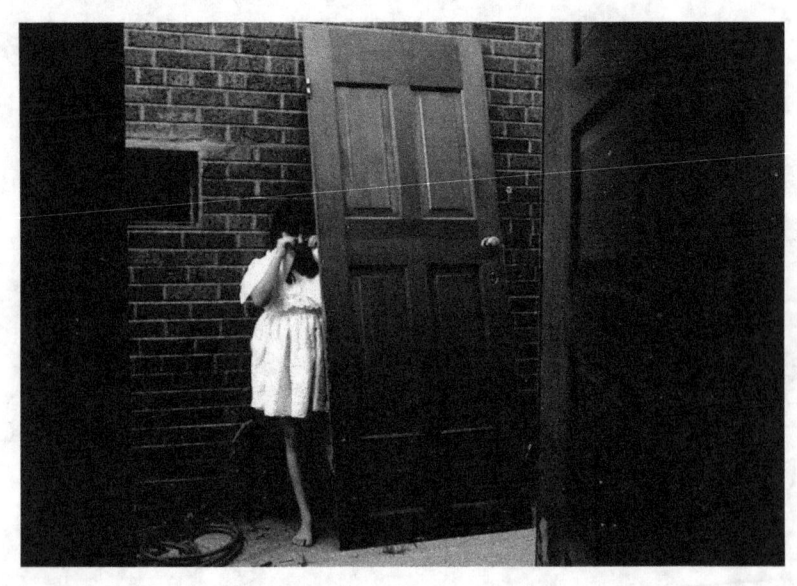

"Desolate Doorway"

# Illinois

# Autumn

# 2005

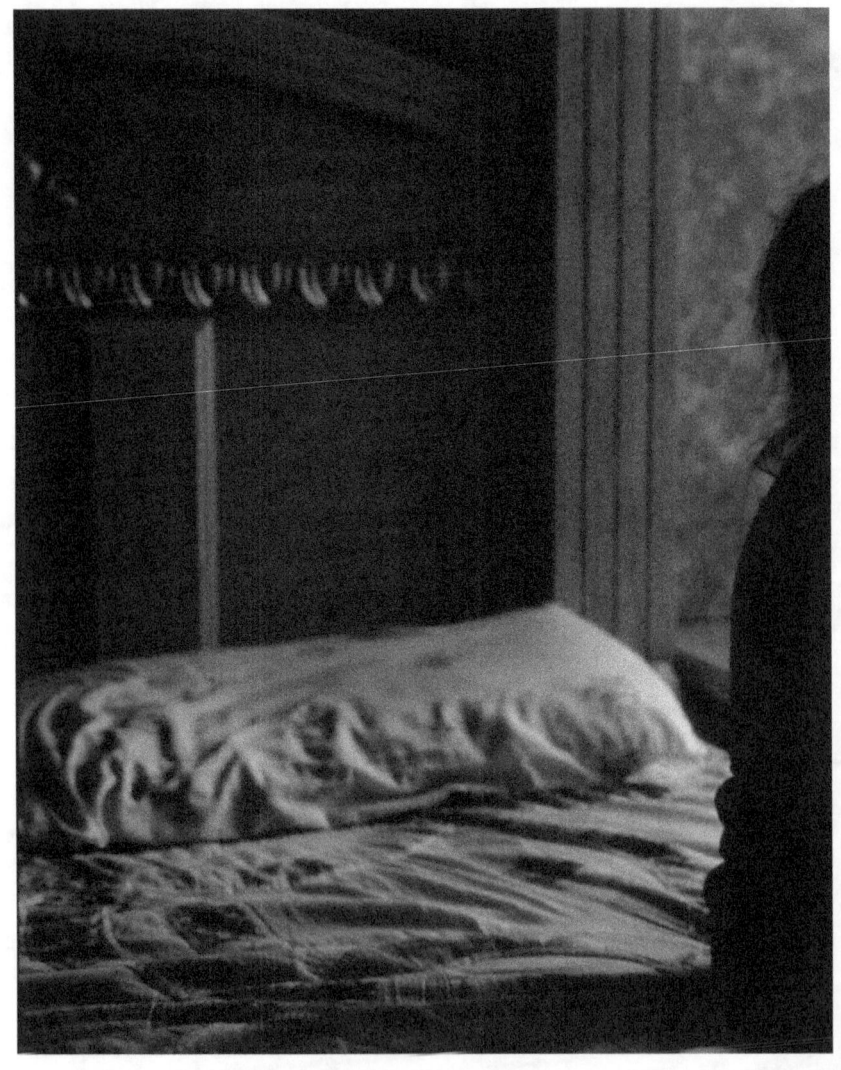

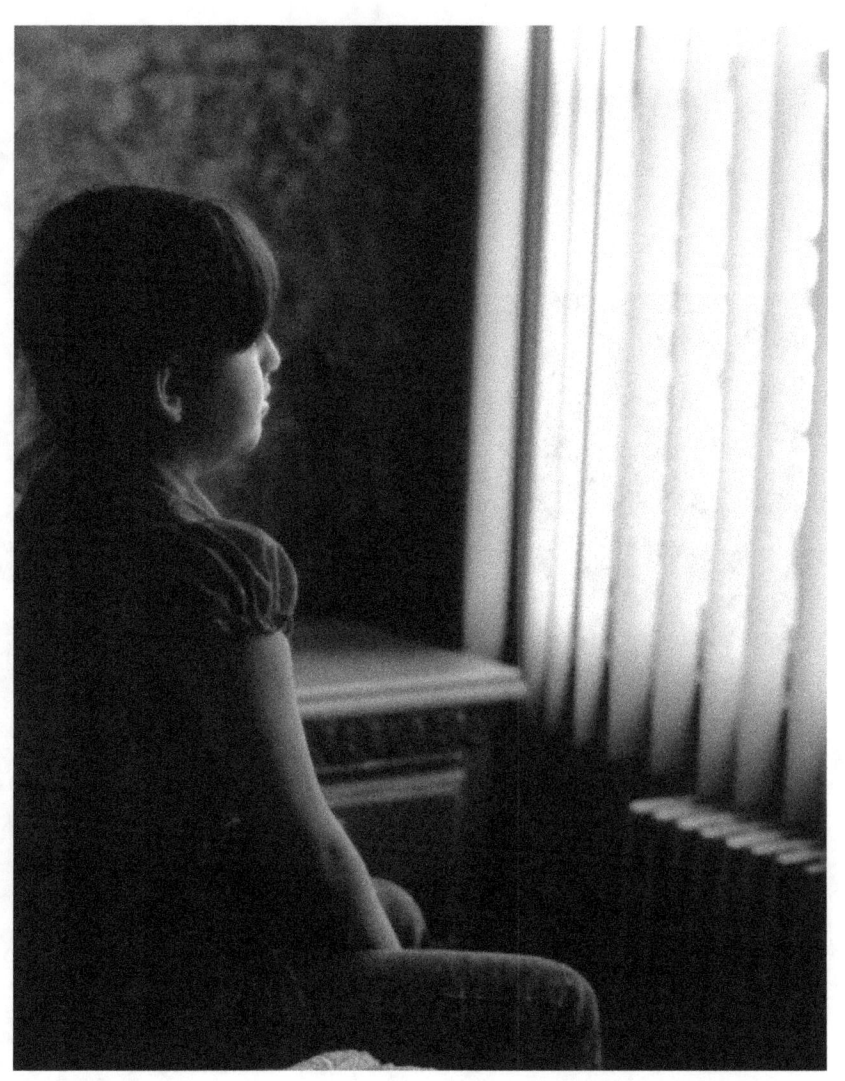

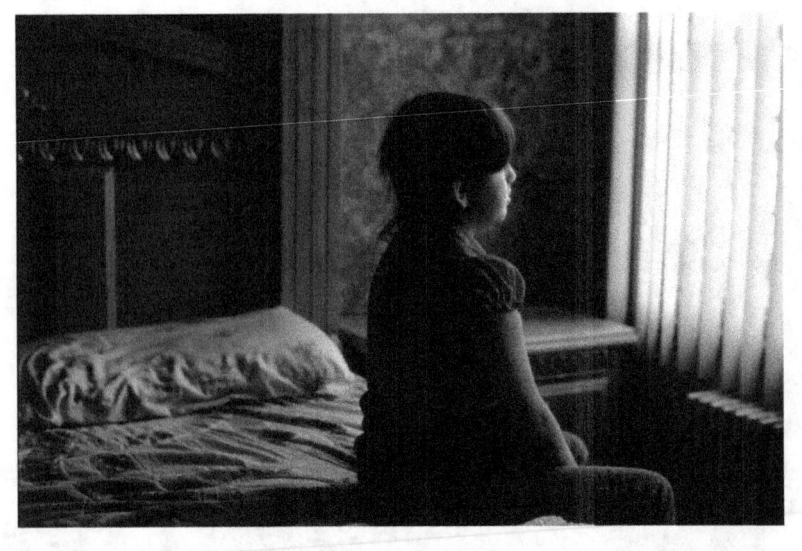

## "Ponder Place"

# Illinois
# Autumn
# 2006

# "Summer Starlight"

# 05162006

Soon our peacefulness will reside
A gracious eternity
When we find ourselves side by side
The scenic serenity
Of the starry night we collide
An untamed destiny

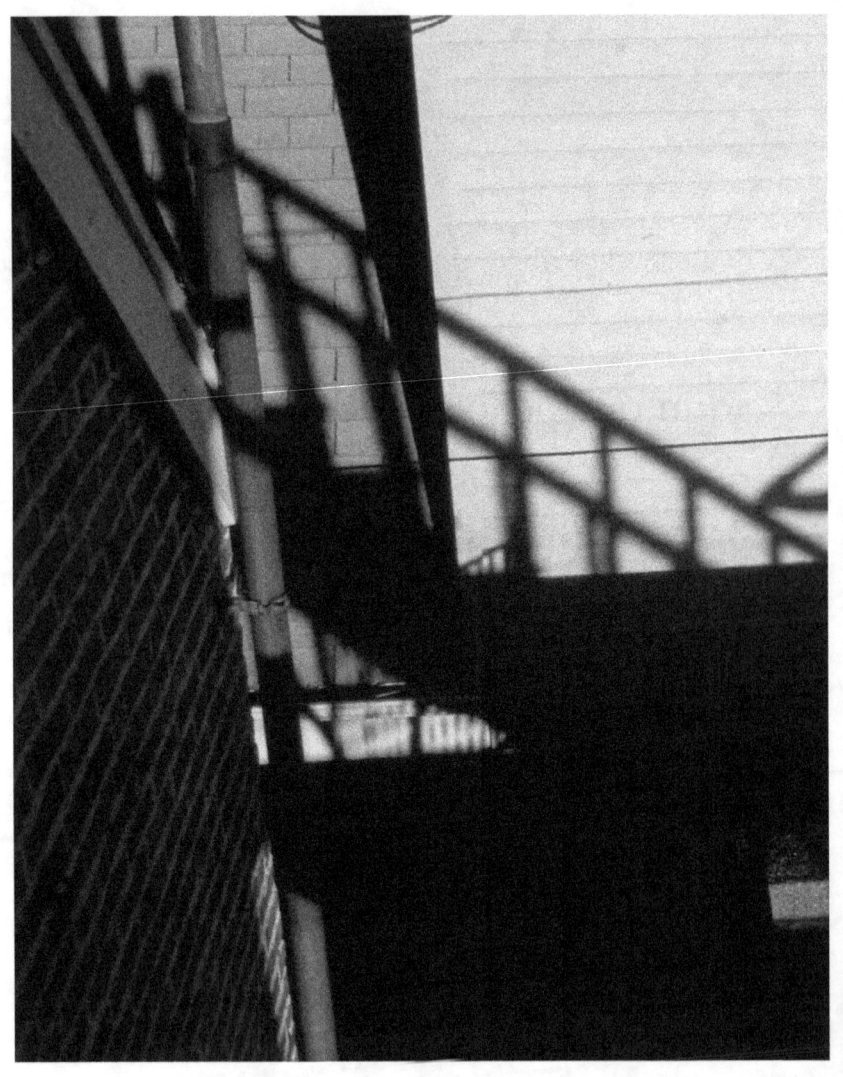

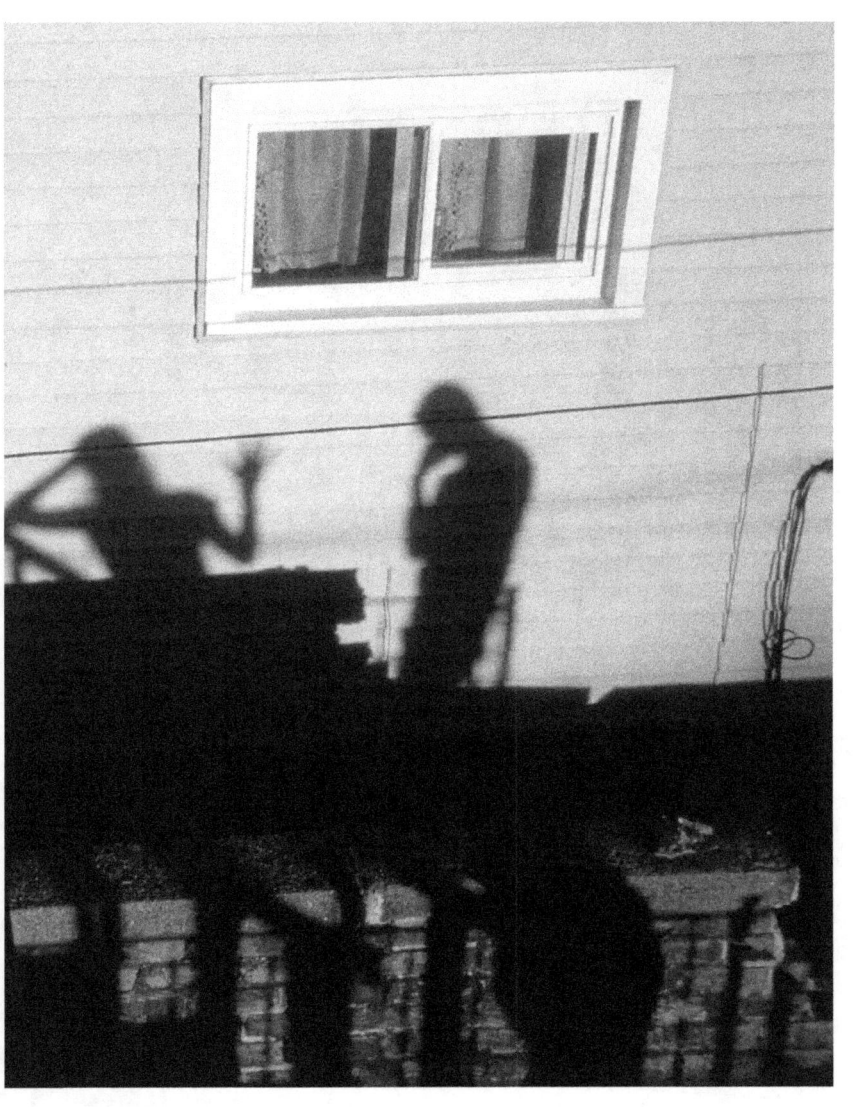

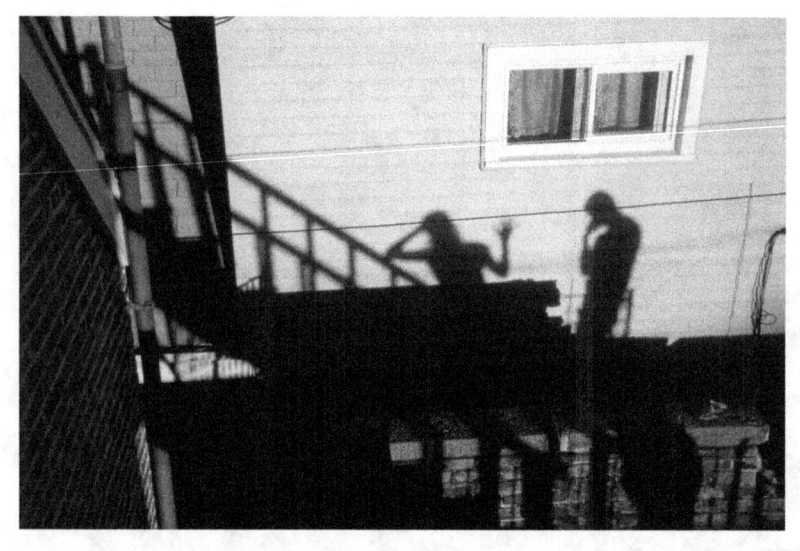

"Shadow Sunset"

# Illinois

# Autumn

# 2005

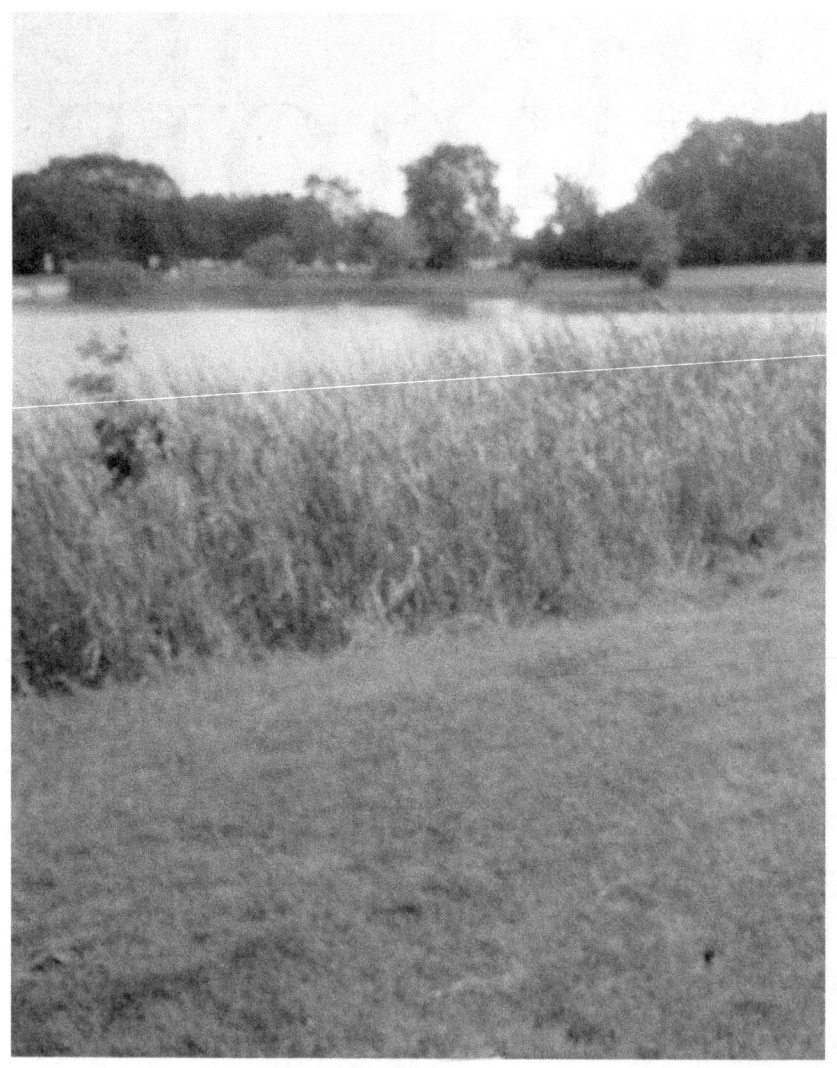

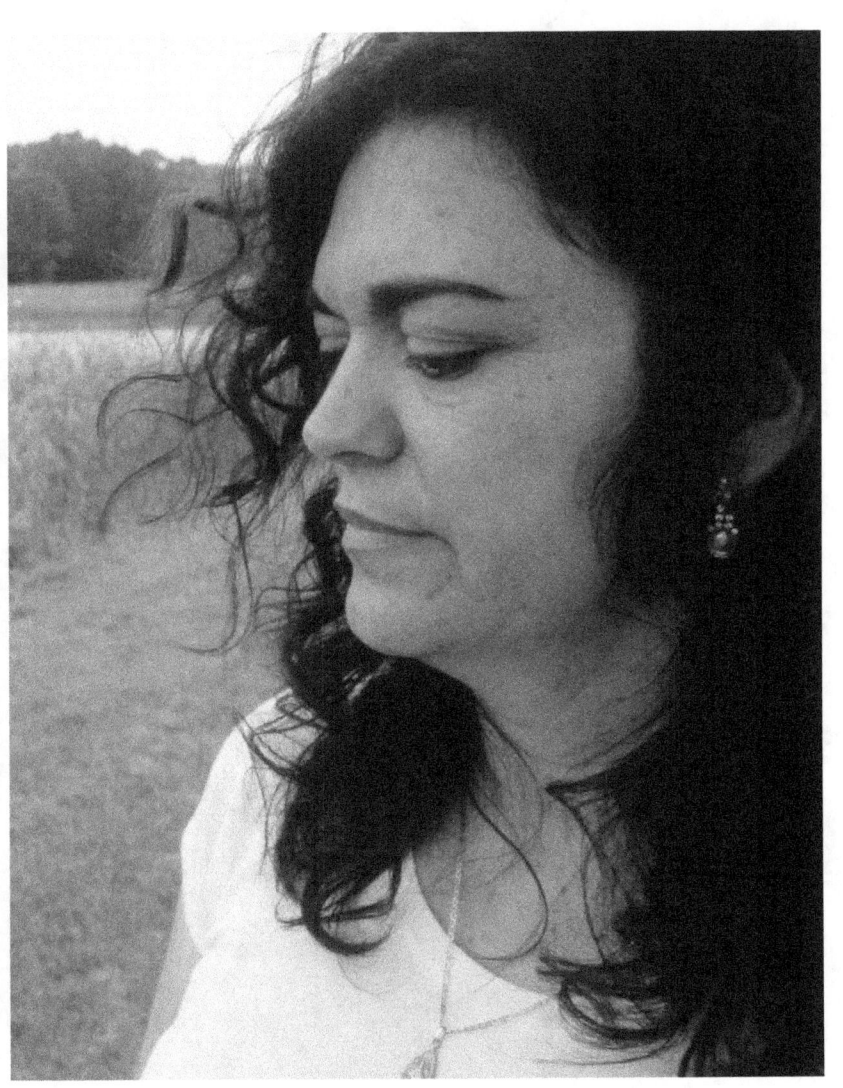

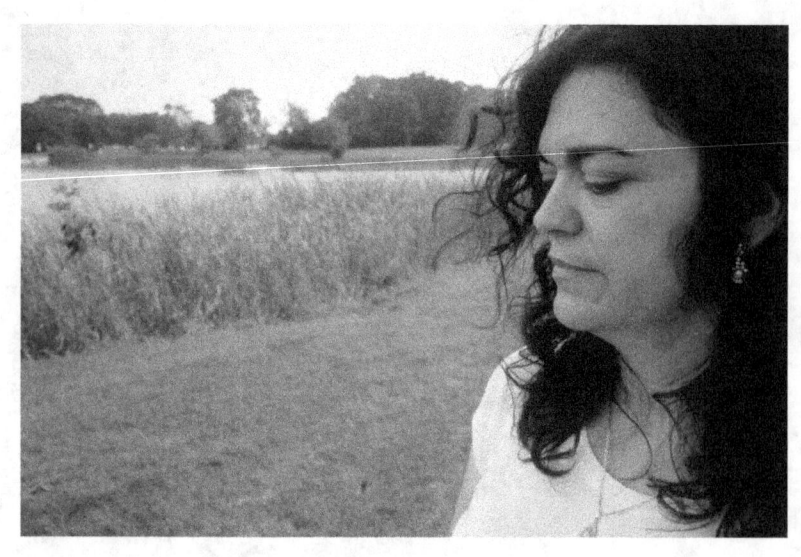

# "Bailarina Bella"

# Illinois

# Summer

# 2006

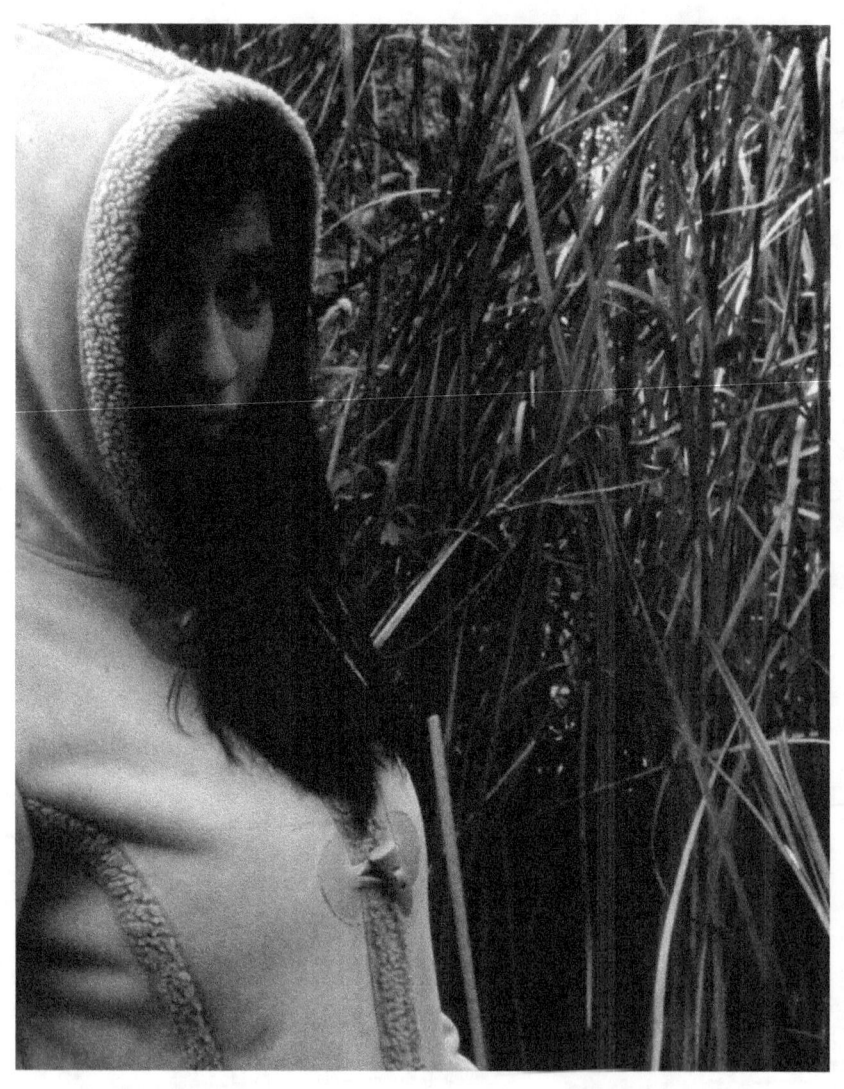

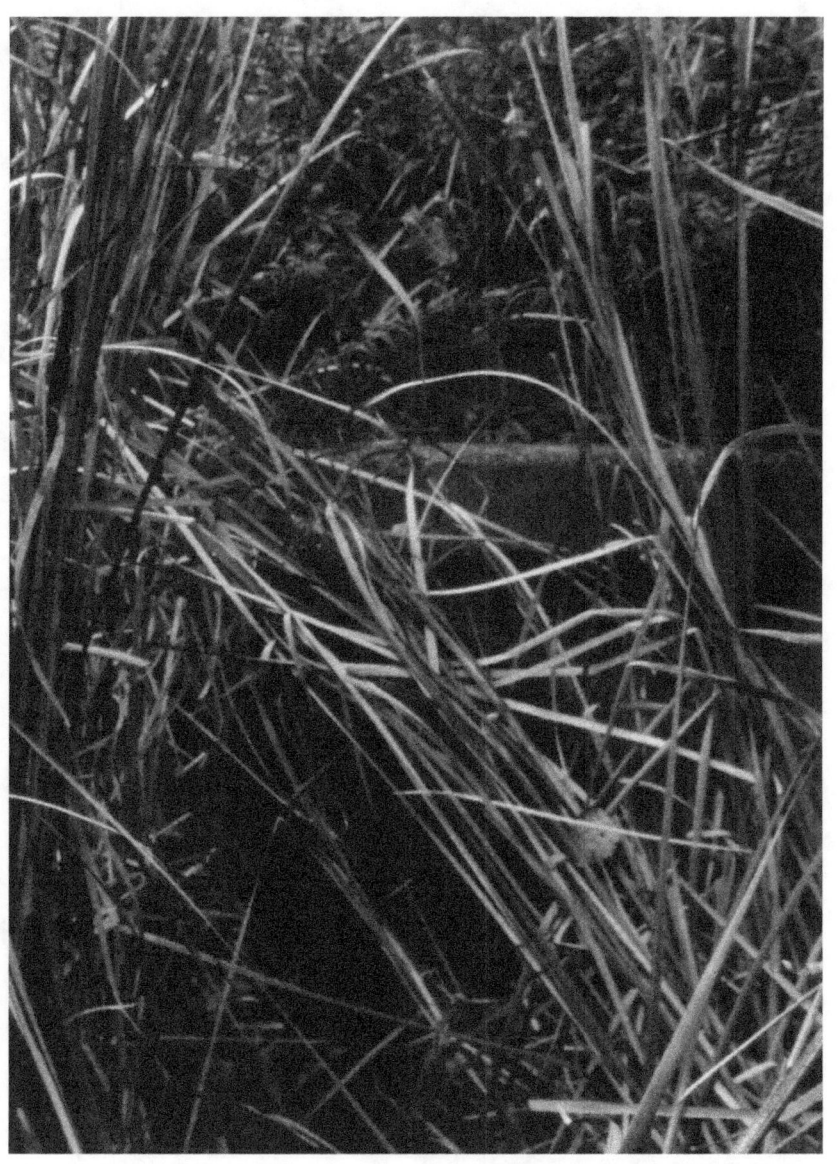

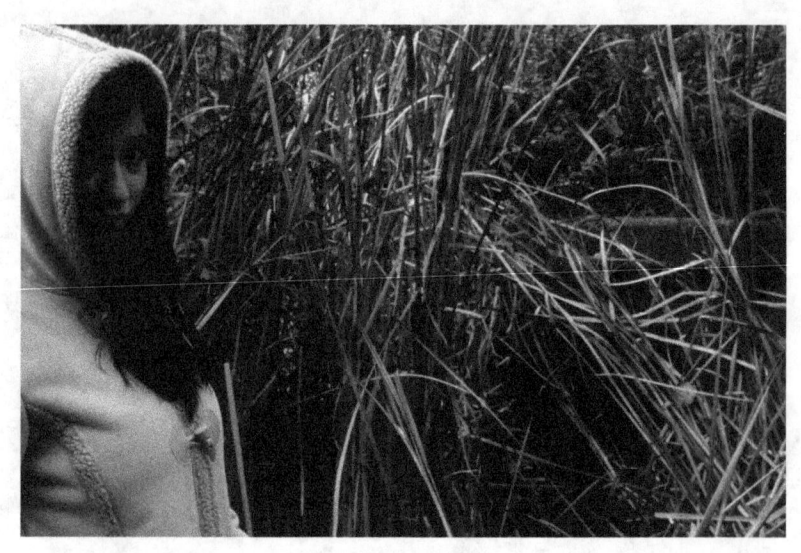

# "Wonder Weeds"

# Illinois

# Autumn

# 2006

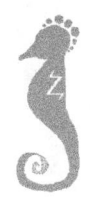

# Zmurbi Librumz

## About The Author
## Zuqy Cruz Marquez

Zuqy took most of these photographs at the age of twenty-two.
They are a Brujx who enjoys the magic of art creation.
They invite to you do the same.

# <u>Zmurbi Librumz</u>
## Publishing Haus

11: A Kidstory Book (The Decennium Series)
22: A Poetimagery Book (The Decennium Series)
02022021: Poetry Gallery (The Gallery Series)
Thallus: Twenty-Two Treatments
these twenty-two teeny tomes (Z&Q Book One)
zQz Magazine: Volume One

amor
armonia
arte

www.ingramcontent.com/pod-product-compliance
Lightning Source LLC
Chambersburg PA
CBHW070437180526
45158CB00019B/1511